WITHDRAWN
UTSA LIBRARIES

SOUTH AFRICA A CENTURY AGO

TO

THE VISCOUNTESS MELVILLE

I DEDICATE THIS BOOK

The Lady Anne Barnard
From a miniature by Cosway.

SOUTH AFRICA A CENTURY AGO

LETTERS WRITTEN
FROM THE CAPE OF GOOD HOPE

(1797–1801)

BY

THE LADY ANNE BARNARD

EDITED WITH A MEMOIR AND BRIEF NOTES
BY
W. H. WILKINS, M.A., F.S.A.

WITH A PORTRAIT

LONDON: SMITH, ELDER, & CO.
NEW YORK: DODD, MEAD, & CO.
1901

Republished 1972
Scholarly Press, Inc., 22929 Industrial Drive East
St. Clair Shores, Michigan 48080

Library of Congress Cataloging in Publication Data

Barnard, Lady Anne (Lindsay) 1750-1825.
  South Africa a century ago.

  1. Cape of Good Hope--History. 2. Cape of Good
Hope--Description and travel. I. Title.
DT844.25.B2A3 1972   916.8'7   71-116271
ISBN 0-403-00461-6

PREFACE

THE letters which form this book were written by Lady Anne Barnard from Cape Colony to the first Viscount Melville, then the Right Honourable Henry Dundas, Secretary of State for War, Treasurer of the Navy, and President of the Board of Control in Pitt's first Administration, during the earliest British occupation of South Africa, a century ago.

These letters remained among the archives at Melville Castle for a hundred years. They are now published by permission of the present Lord Melville, to whom the manuscripts belong. There is no need to dwell upon the peculiar fitness of their publication at the present time, when South African affairs loom large in men's minds. But the circumstances under which they were written lend to them an especial interest. They are not merely the letters of a clever woman to her intimate friend, but those of the wife of the first Secretary of Cape Colony to the Secretary of State at home. Lord Melville was the Minister chiefly responsible for the annexation of Cape Colony by the English. Almost alone among British statesmen, he early recognised the importance of our keeping the Cape, not only because of its value as a station on the road to India, but because of the internal resources of the Colony and its great possibilities of development. He called the Cape his 'favourite child,' he watched over it with unflagging zeal, and he resigned office rather than be a party to its cession to the Dutch.[1] He appointed Lord Macartney first Governor of Cape Colony, and Mr. Barnard, Lady Anne's husband, Secretary. The charm, talent, and rare social qualities of Lady Anne Barnard led Lord Melville to give this appointment to her husband. The Governor's wife (Lady Macartney) was not accompanying her husband; the wife of the Secretary would therefore be the first lady of the Colony, and have to perform many of the social duties which usually fall to the lot of the Governor's wife. Lady Anne was ad-

---

[1] As a small illustration of this I may mention that in the library at Melville Castle there is an old volume entitled *Walks and Sketches at the Cape of Good Hope*, by Robert Temple, 1803. It is dedicated to the first Lord Melville, and in the dedication the writer says: 'I have been induced to request the permission of affixing your lordship's name hereto, solely from the conviction that no man in Great Britain has paid so much attention to the affairs of the Cape, or has so intimate an acquaintance with every subject relative to that Colony, as your lordship.'

mirably fitted to fill such a position, and she enjoyed the friendship and confidence of the Secretary of State in no ordinary degree. Lord Melville charged her to conciliate the Dutch as much as possible, and to write to him freely about everything that occurred. These letters will show how well she fulfilled his wishes in both respects. They cover the period of the Administrations of the first two English Governors (Lord Macartney and Sir George Yonge), and, in addition to giving vivid descriptions of South Africa at that time, they are full of shrewd observations and wise suggestions as to the government of the Colony, especially with regard to the treatment of the natives and the conciliation of the Dutch. The student of history will note, too, that many of the same problems presented themselves for solution a century ago in South Africa as present themselves to-day; the same difficulties arose, and perhaps the same mistakes were committed on either side.

Lady Anne Barnard was also the authoress of the ever-popular ballad *Auld Robin Gray*, and one of the best-known figures in the literary and social world of her day. Her fascinating personality is all too little known. I have therefore prefaced her letters from South Africa with a brief memoir, and have incorporated in it certain other letters which she wrote from Ireland and elsewhere. They reveal, like everything else she wrote, the same sterling qualities—a keen perception, a liberal mind, a warm heart, and a magnetic gift of sympathy.

I take this opportunity of acknowledging my indebtedness to LORD MELVILLE not only for his permission to publish this correspondence, but for much valuable aid and kind encouragement. I have also to thank MR. G. FYDELL ROWLEY and MRS. ATHOLL FORBES for leave to reproduce the miniature of Lady Anne Barnard by Cosway as a frontispiece.

W. H. WILKINS.

MEMOIR

MEMOIR

LADY ANNE LINDSAY (by marriage Barnard) was the eldest child of James, fifth Earl of Balcarres, by his wife Anne Dalrymple, daughter of Sir Robert Dalrymple, of Castletown. Both her parents were remarkable. Her father was a brave soldier and a learned and courteous gentleman. He had drawn his sword in the Stuart cause in the rising of 1715, but as the House of Hanover settled itself upon the throne he was too good a patriot not to sink faction for the good of his country, and he fought against its enemies under King George II. at the battle of Dettingen. He lived through troublous times. Born the year after the abdication of King James II., he survived for about twenty years the last effort of the Stuarts to regain their hereditary kingdom in 1745. Branch after branch had been shorn away from his family, until at the time of his marriage Lord Balcarres was the chief of his clan and the last of his race. He was sixty years of age when he married Miss Dalrymple, a lady nearly forty years his junior, beautiful, clever, and endowed with an almost masculine strength of mind, though somewhat lacking in the feminine virtues of softness and charity.

Lady Anne, the first issue of this union, was born December 12, 1750, at Balcarres. Prince Charles Edward and the rising of '45 were still fresh in men's minds; and when it was known that Lady Balcarres was like to be brought to bed, great things were expected of the probable heir of this ancient house. To quote Lady Anne's own words: 'There long existed a prophecy that the first child of the last descendant of the House of Balcarres was to restore the family of Stuart to those hereditary rights which the bigotry of James had deprived them of. The Jacobites seemed to have gained new life on the occasion; the wizards and witches of the period found it in their books; the devil had mentioned it to one or two of his particular friends; old ladies had read it from the grounds of their coffee—no wonder that the event was welcomed with the gasp of expiring hope. Songs were made by exulting Tories, masses were offered up by good Catholics, who longed to see the Pope's bull once more tossing his horns in the country. . . . In due course of time the partisans of the "Pretender," the soothsayers, wizards, witches, the bards, fortune-tellers, and old ladies, were all in a group dismayed, disconcerted, and enraged to learn that Lady Balcarres was brought to bed of a daughter after all, absolutely but a daughter. . . . That child was the Anne Lindsay who now addresses you.'

Lady Anne was not destined to be for long the sole representative of the younger generation of the House of Balcarres, for within the next twelve years the Countess presented her lord with ten other children. To again quote Lady Anne: 'Our excellent parents, having nothing else to do in the country, desisted not from their laudable aim of populating the castle of Balcarres, till their family consisted of eight boys and three girls. Such are the wonders (I speak to all old bachelors) produced by a life of temperance, with the blessing of God.'

Lady Anne was carefully, if somewhat strictly, brought up. Her mother was a martinet with her numerous brood, and ruled her children rather by fear than love, after the fashion of many parents in the eighteenth century. Lord Balcarres gave up the management of his family to his wife, except that when punishments were unduly severe and peccadilloes treated as crimes he would sometimes break in with a remonstrance: 'Odds fish, Madame! you will break the spirits of my young troops; I will not have it so.' Lady Balcarres used to say that Anne was the most difficult to punish of all her children, since her shortcomings were not sufficient to earn her a whipping. Margaret, who was Lady Anne's favourite sister, and two years younger, was of a much more high-spirited temperament and was generally in revolt and in disgrace. On one occasion Lady Margaret assembled the other children together, and proposed flight in consequence of the 'horrious' life they suffered at home. The proposal was carried with acclamation, and the six children set off forthwith, but their escape was retarded by little James, who was not yet breeched, and whom they had to carry in turns. They had not gone far when their flight was discovered by old Robin Gray, the shepherd, who went to Lady Balcarres with the news: 'All the young gentlemen and the young ladies and all the dogs are run away, my lady.' The truants were soon captured and brought back, and the punishment of each this time was a dose of tincture of rhubarb in varying degree.

Lady Anne was given a good education in keeping with her social position—in fact, rather in advance of it, as education for women was understood in that day—and as she grew up she showed signs that she had inherited a full share of the family talents. Her childhood was spent at Balcarres, but as she became older visits were frequently paid to Edinburgh, to the house of her grandmother, Lady Dalrymple, or to Sir Thomas Oughton's country house outside the city. Lady Dalrymple, a clever old lady, was intimate with many of the most eminent Scotsmen of her time. Among her friends was David Hume, the historian, whom she had known from a child. Lady Anne mentions him in a letter which she wrote to her sister Margaret about this time from her grandmother's house in Edinburgh. 'Dinners go on as usual,' she wrote, 'which being monopolised by the divines, wits and writers of the present day, are not unjustly called "the dinners of the *caterati*" by Lord Kellie, who laughs at his own pun until his face is purple. Our friend David Hume, along with his friend Principal Robertson, continue to maintain their ground at these convivial meetings. To see the lion and the lamb lying down together, the deist and the doctor, is extraordinary; it makes one hope that some day Hume will say to him, "Thou almost persuadest me to be a Christian." He is a constant visitor of ours.'

When Lady Anne was in her twenty-first year her sister, Lady Margaret, was married to Mr. Alexander Fordyce, of Roehampton. Lady Margaret's charms and mental accomplishments were recorded by many of her admiring contemporaries.

Her beauty inspired Sheridan with the well-known lines:

> Mark'd you her eye of heavenly blue,
> Mark'd you her cheek of rosy hue;
> That eye in liquid circles roving,
> That cheek abashed at man's approving.
> The one love's arrows darting round,
> The other blushing at the wound.

It was soon after her sister's marriage, in 1771, that Lady Anne wrote the ballad which will ever remain her title to fame. Bereft of the companionship of her sister, she was driven back on her own resources, and her literary talents began to make themselves manifest. 'Residing,' she says, 'in the solitude of the country, without other sources of entertainment but what I could draw from myself, I used to mount up to my little closet in the high winding staircase, which commanded the sea, the lake, the rocks, the birds, the beach, and with my pen in my hand and a few envelopes of old letters, which too often vanished afterwards, scribbled away poetically and in prose.' It was on one of these occasions that 'Auld Robin Gray' was written.[1] For some unaccountable reason she never publicly acknowledged the authorship until 1823, two years

---

[1] The original text of *Auld Robin Gray* is given in an appendix to this memoir. Lady Anne wrote a sequel or continuation to it some years later, but, like many sequels, it is inferior to the original.

before her death; indeed, it seems that she denied having written it, for once when on a visit at Dalkeith, Lady Jane Scott, sister of the Duke of Buccleuch, said: 'You sing that song in a way that makes me sure it is your own writing.' Lady Anne, according to her own statement, blushed scarlet, and denied it. 'Do not do so,' said Lady Jane; 'I will betray you unless you give me a copy of it.' Lady Anne says: 'To convince her I was not the author, I gave her a copy, entreating her not to let anybody have it.' But Lady Jane copied it for her friends, and soon the song got out into the world, and became widely popular, though its authorship remained a disputed point.

A few years after Lord Balcarres died Lady Anne left Balcarres and went to live in Edinburgh with her mother, the Dowager-Countess, who had taken a house there. In Edinburgh she mixed freely in the literary society for which the northern capital was famous. When Johnson came to Edinburgh in 1773 he was introduced to Lady Anne, who had gathered round her a numerous company of friends, including Hume, McKenzie, and Monboddo. It was probably about this time that she made the acquaintance of Henry Dundas, then a rising young Scottish politician, who had been appointed, at the age of twenty-four, Solicitor-

General for Scotland, and for whom his Edinburgh friends already predicted a brilliant career. Lady Anne had a great respect and affection for her mother, but she was not particularly happy with her, and after the death of Mr. Fordyce she went to London to reside with her widowed sister, Lady Margaret Fordyce, who had taken one of the smaller houses in Berkeley Square. There the two sisters lived together for many years. The beauty of Lady Margaret, and the charm and lively conversation of Lady Anne, 'one of the most fascinating women of her time,' as a contemporary describes her, made them very popular, and their house became a social centre, and a favourite resort of some of the most famous literary and political men of the day. Pitt, Burke, Sheridan, Windham, and Dundas are a few of those who were wont to avail themselves of the sisters' simple yet charming hospitality; the Prince of Wales was also one of their frequent guests, and his friendship with Lady Anne lasted all his life. They also enjoyed a considerable share of Court favour from King George and Queen Charlotte. 'The Lindsay sisters,' as they were called, occupied a unique position in the London society of their day.

With such opportunities Lady Anne, it may readily be believed, had many offers, some of them exceptionally good, but she refused them all. The reason that she remained unwed all these years is ascribed by her nephew, Colonel Lindsay, to indecision (in other matters it seems to have formed no part of her character) and to a reluctance to leave her sister. But the 'Melville Letters,' hitherto unpublished, afford, I think, a clue to the mystery. Lady Anne's heart was really given to Henry Dundas, with whom, to the day of his death, she remained on terms of intimate friendship. Dundas was now one of the first statesmen of the day, the most powerful man in Scotland, the intimate friend and trusted lieutenant of Pitt, a great Parliamentary debater, and a successful Minister. His career excited the admiration of his friends, and of none more than Lady Anne. But though Dundas attained public greatness, he was unfortunate in his private relations. His beautiful first wife, daughter and heiress of David Rennie, of Melville Castle, deserted him for another man; a divorce followed, and it was some years before Dundas took to himself another wife. In private life he was of a free and genial disposition, fond of ladies' society, and during those years when his public career was at its zenith, but his domestic happiness broken up, he was a frequent and welcome guest at the sisters' house in Berkeley Square. He sought eagerly the society of Lady Anne, taking her into his confidence, and talking to

her unreservedly about political and private matters.
Whether he ever contemplated marriage with her,
or led her to believe that he did, it is impossible to
say; but it is certain that Lady Anne became very
much attached to him. The news that he was going
to marry Lady Jane Hope, the daughter of the
second Earl of Hopetoun, must have come to her
as a blow.

Whatever Lady Anne suffered, she kept her
feelings to herself. She showed no disposition to
wear the willow, and in 1793 astonished her friends
by marrying Mr. Andrew Barnard, son of the Bishop
of Limerick. The marriage, from a worldly point of
view, could hardly be considered other than im-
prudent. Lady Anne was forty-three years of age,
her husband was fifteen years her junior; he had been
in the Army; he was good-looking, well-mannered, of
moderate ability and amiable disposition. It is only
fair to say that, despite the disparity of age, he made
Lady Anne a very good husband, and she grew to
be much attached to him. The problem of ways
and means early presented itself. Barnard had a
small patrimony and many debts; Lady Anne had
little or nothing. But she was always of a sanguine disposition, and she looked forward to obtaining for her husband a Government appointment of
some kind through the influence of her highly placed

friends. Her most intimate friend was Dundas, now Secretary for War, Treasurer of the Navy, and President of the Board of Control in Pitt's First Administration, and to him she applied. A few months after her marriage she went to Ireland with her husband to make the acquaintance of his relatives, and from there we find her writing to Dundas:

'I have not forgotten, my dear friend, what you hinted to me in confidence respecting the possibility of Mr. Barnard deriving a benefit from a situation ostensibly given to another, and to be sure this would be a very eligible favour for our interests, and one I should most gratefully thank you for. But until this occurs, will you contrive to place him in any office, with no matter how little salary, where he might have something to do and prove himself useful? He was pleased with your manner to him, and said he had never talked to a great man who had so much the power of making a man, who was asking a favour, feel at ease with him as yourself. If you could place him on your own Board, or anywhere where he might gain your friendship by deserving it, and by being connected with yourself, he would be glad. But I put the matter into your hands and leave it. You will find a mode of serving us; the sooner you can do so in any shape the better.

I prefer owing to you than to any other person, because I can never cease to have for you sentiments which make the feeling of gratitude sit easy in my heart.'[1]

But good appointments, real or sinecure, even in those days, were not to be had for the asking, and though Dundas renewed his promise, no suitable vacancy occurred. In 1794, in consequence of a rumour that her powerful friend was about to retire from the Government, Lady Anne again wrote from Ireland to renew her request :

'On an occasion so important as this, I think it right for me to remind you of myself, depending on your kindness, so many proofs of which I have experienced on former occasions, and almost certain that distance would not make you forget the hearty assurance you gave me of assisting my husband. I have never teased you about it, because I committed my interests wholly into your hands, while I formed all my counsels here on the confidence I have in you, in consequence of what passed between you and me the last time I saw you, which I naturally repeated to Mr. Barnard. I prevailed on him to give up the Army, though considerable advantages were offered him by the Lord Lieutenant,

[1] Letter from Lady Anne Barnard to the Right Hon. Henry Dundas, St. Wolstan's, near Dublin, December 10, 1793.

as he has been seventeen years in the Army, and has served many years abroad. I have also prevailed on him and his family to consent to our letting St. Wolstan's for a term of years, almost the prettiest place in Ireland, but one which our income did not render it eligible to keep, and to have a house in London also. To indulge me these things have been done. Am I not therefore doubly bound, my dear friend, to use every exertion which zeal, duty, and gratitude can give, with a friend who has long been mine, who knows our situation, and who, I trust, will not on this occasion desert me, to replace to my husband the pleasures of which I have deprived him, to secure my own comfort amongst my own friends? I throw myself on you with earnestness and hope; *you owe me some happiness, in truth you do.* Pay me by making me the means of serving a man who has rebuilt in a considerable degree what tumbled to its foundation, who makes my happiness his study, and whose prospects in this country (Ireland) have been given up for me.'[1]

Still nothing was forthcoming, though Dundas remained in office. In truth, Barnard, who had few qualifications, was not an easy man to fit with a

[1] Letter from Lady Anne Barnard to the Right Hon. Henry Dundas, St. Wolstan's, near Dublin, March 10, 1794.

suitable appointment. After waiting another year, Lady Anne came over to England to see what pleading in person would do. She saw the powerful Minister; Dundas had not forgotten, and renewed his promises. Lady Anne followed up the interview by writing him a still more strongly worded letter:

'Do not let me, my dear friend, return to Ireland dispirited, and have to tell the Bishop and Mrs. Barnard that the flattering hopes I gave them for their son, from the kind promises you made me previous to our marriage three years ago, have not been realised. I have explained myself fully to you, and refer to our conversation once again to implore you to ask your own heart whether you ought not to feel yourself doubly bound to make my situation comfortable, more than you are bound to any other woman in this world. To a man like you, generous as well as just, how many motives are there not in the strong, though defeated, regards which have subsisted between us, for you to take my husband by the hand, and make me, through him, as happy as you can? To pay me all you have owed, and still owe me, you *never* can. But what you can you should do, and you have got before you the pleasure of obliging me. I have paid you tears of gratitude for the hearty manner in which you pledged yourself to serve us, and while I have any memory I must depend on your doing so, but hope deferred maketh the heart sick.'[1]

This last appeal had its effect. On the conquest of the Cape of Good Hope, the Home Government determined to send out Lord Macartney as Governor, and Dundas offered the appointment of Secretary of the Colony to Mr. Barnard, with a salary of 3,500*l.* a year. Barnard was delighted with the appointment, as he ought to have been, but Lady Anne demurred somewhat. The idea of banishment to an unknown land, as the Cape then was, rather frightened her; she would have preferred, she told Dundas, a situation with less emolument nearer home, and she was not quite sure whether the post of Secretary was not one beneath Mr. Barnard's acceptance; or, rather, whether the position of Secretary's wife was one suitable for her rank. All these doubts and fears she communicated by letter. Dundas answered her shortly, saying that it was the 'prettiest appointment in the world for any young fellow,' and telling her that she must take that or nothing. He had some reason to be hurt, for he had given this appointment to Barnard, a young and untried man, solely because of his goodwill for his wife. He had thoughtfully chosen it also because (as Lady Macartney was not

[1] Letter from Lady Anne Barnard to the Right Hon. Henry Dundas, London, April 30, 1796.

going out to the Cape) Lady Anne would be able to play the part of first lady in the Colony and represent the Government, which he knew she would like. Lady Anne, fearing that she had offended her powerful friend, apologised with tears, and a reconciliation was effected between them. In March 1797 she and her husband left England with Lord Macartney for the Cape, where they arrived, on board the 'Trusty,' on May 4, 1797, and took over the Government of the Colony.

The record of Lady Anne's life in South Africa is told in full in the letters which are published in this book, so we will not allude to it at length here. Her letters were all written to Dundas, and the fact that he tied them together and kept them carefully preserved among his most cherished papers at Melville Castle shows that the great Minister, through all his vicissitudes, kept a soft corner in his heart for Lady Anne.

On the cession of the Cape to the Dutch by the Peace of Amiens, Lady Anne came back to England in 1802; her husband followed her a few months later. Lady Anne tried hard to obtain for Barnard another Government appointment, but without success. The Pitt Ministry was come to an end; her powerful friend, Dundas (now Lord Melville), had resigned office rather than be a party to the ignoble Peace, and Addington turned a deaf ear to her representations. Baffled in her endeavours, she went to Ireland, where a new vexation awaited her in the fact that her father-in-law, the Bishop of Limerick, who was now a widower, at the age of seventy-six, declared his intention of marrying a young girl. The scandal and annoyance this occasioned to his relatives may be imagined. After trying in vain to put matters right, Lady Anne went on to visit her brother-in-law and sister, Lord and Lady Hardwicke, at Dublin Castle.

Lord Hardwicke was then Lord Lieutenant of Ireland, and the time was critical. The Irish Catholics were indignant, and rightly, at the disappointment of their hopes of emancipation, which Pitt had promised to give them, but the King refused. The discontent which had brought about the Irish Rebellion of 1798 under Lord Edward FitzGerald was still rife, and the return to Ireland of exiles from France after the Peace of Amiens had enabled Napoleon to establish negotiations with the Irish malcontents. Fortunately, Napoleon and the French were now unpopular with the Irish Catholics on account of Napoleon's treatment of the Pope, and the great body of them held aloof. A rising took place, but instead of being national it was confined to a small number of Protestant republicans, and hardly exceeded the proportions of a town riot. Emmett, the leader, was taken and executed. Lady Anne was staying at the Castle through this troublous time, and she wrote a letter to Lord Melville, from which we take the following extract:

'As I think that, retired as you are amongst your own mountains, surrounded by your own friends, your own faithful Highlanders, eating your own mutton and drinking your own ale, you will not be sorry to know what is going on in this agitated country, separated from our native land by so little, I take up my pen to give you, my dear friend, a little of such Irish news as is on the cards at present. Alas! that I must write to you so much of trials, rebels, and matters of the baneful, alarming, and horrid kind, of which Ireland is full at present. I want to tell you, though, before I begin on these sad things, that Lord Hardwicke reviewed the different corps a few days ago, about five thousand, in the Phœnix Park. They made a very respectable appearance; the commanding officers all dined here afterwards in St. Patrick's Hall, which, together with the good dinner and sumptuous service of plate, made also a very good appearance of a different sort.

'You will, I know, expect to hear something of the

trials and executions of the poor, faulty, and deluded men, whose guilt cannot admit of doubt, which have been taking place. Several have been hanged in the eyes of a great concourse of people, who have shown no disposition to question or to rescue. There are, however, in spite of oneself, many circumstances which daily take place, while such solemn scenes are going forward, to freeze the blood and sometimes to awaken pity for youth and talents so perverted. I refer especially to Emmett, the misguided leader of this unhappy matter. Emmett was the son of a physician, only twenty-three, as I believe, and of great, though perverted, talents. I must tell you of the reply of the young woman who was taken at the same time, and who wore green ribbons in her hat, the rebel colour. "Why," said the officer, "is it that so pretty a young woman as you wear this object of sedition?" She coldly answered, "You can't help the colour, do what you will; it grows every day." There is a very singular story in circulation here, which I fancy is not without foundation, that the daughter of Curran, the famous counsellor, was in correspondence with Emmett, and it is said that her love-letters found on him, mixed with politics, were fatal to him. No one believes that Curran, her father, knew of this correspondence; he some time ago changed his doctrines, and declared himself loyal for the future. "It was more to his interest," he said, "as he had a rising family." He was to have been counsel for Emmett, but on this discovery declined it, and still refuses to see his daughter. The young man was said to have behaved extraordinarily well.

'I think you will like to know the result of Emmett's trial and the manner in which he quitted his busy and turbulent career. The Court was crowded at a very early hour. The trial began at nine o'clock and lasted till eight in the evening. Many men went there with a considerable mixture of compassion for his youth and perverted talents, but these sentiments did not remain; the proofs of his guilt were so clear that at his own desire his counsel did not make any defence. Some extracts only of the letters I mentioned were read, and the name was withheld. It is said that these letters were the principal evidence to condemn him. The name was withheld, I clearly saw, in delicacy to the young woman's father, Mr. Curran, who has lately become the friend of the Government, and has the ability to do much harm. The behaviour of Emmett during the trial was cool, firm, and manly. After he was found guilty he spoke at considerable length, it was thought in a daring and improper manner, avowing his principles and glorying in them. I do not, however, think his speech reads *ill*; to be sure, it is daring and impetuous, but I think it is sincere, and the speech of a republican and an enthusiast, who from infancy imbibed a set of false doctrines which an ardent and ambitious mind formed, and a low-placed attachment riveted.

'When Lord Norbury told Emmett that he had been found guilty of high treason, and asked him why the sentence of the law should not be passed on him, he replied:

'" My Lord, with respect to the trial and the verdict pronounced, nothing ; but with respect to some of the charges this night settled, I have much to say. I have been charged with being an emissary of France. Hear the declaration of a dying man. I say it is false—I never was an emissary of France. I acknowledge that the Provisional Government treated with France, and at this moment an ambassador from this country is in Paris to obtain a treaty signed, before an expedition should sail to get for this country such a constitution as Franklin has obtained for America. I have no faith in treaties. My object was to obtain for the people their rights, to restore what had been wrested from them, to act with the people against the Government to obtain it, but not, as it was construed to-night, by foreign aid. So contrary was my plan that I accelerated the attack of the 23rd, lest the French should arrive. Hear the declaration of a dying man. My views were not formed upon ambitious motives. I had no desire for emolument or aggrandisement. I sacrificed ideals dear to my heart to obtain for the people their rights; I now lose my life for it. Read our proclamation. My wish was to effect this without bloodshed. I declare as a dying man I did not wish to spill blood."

'Here Lord Norbury interrupted him, but Emmett went on: "My Lord, it is true that you are the judge and I am the culprit. My Lord, you are but a man, so am I. I claim nothing as a culprit from a judge. I only desire that my dying request may be granted, and that this may pass with my life, that when I meet the cold grave no epitaph may be written on my tomb. Future times will record the work that I began."

'Here the Judge said this must end, and Emmett concluded: "My Lord, I state the solemn truth, as I shall shortly appear before my God. I was not the author of this movement, but joined it because the sentiments it professed agreed with my own. From the age of ten these sentiments were mine and will go to the grave with me—to join the people against the Government for the redress of their grievances, and were it to be done again to-morrow I would act as I have done. But hear my last declaration. I hate French principles and I hate the French; I see they have paid no respect to treaties. Were I in Switzerland I would join the people against the French; I would do the same here, and would be one of the foremost to fight against them. These are my sentiments; for these I die. My ministry has come to a close."

'After sentence was passed Emmett was by mistake taken to Newgate and lodged in a miserable cell, which being discovered by Mr. Wickham, he sent a strong party of dragoons, and removed him to his former prison, where he was comfortably accommodated until the next day, when he was to be executed. Emmett expressed himself sensible of this mark of attention to the Officer of the Guard, who repeated this, and a good deal more, to me. The doomed man also, in a conversation with the Attorney-General, O'Grady, entered more at large into his views and plans than he had done the day before. He reiterated his abhorrence of the French, their principles, and their government, and said he had been eager to make *his push* before the invasion *they* meditated would make it theirs. He disclaimed private views of ambition or interest, and showed a man burning with a fire which flashed only to mislead, being self-misled. I do not believe that Miss Curran requested to see him; if she did she would not have been permitted. The conduct of Redman, who shot himself, had rendered it necessary that Emmett should be searched in court to prevent his concealing the means of self-destruction, and he was handcuffed. Many letters were found on him which were not exposed, and a lock of hair and a small bunch of valerian. He said to the jailer, "For Heaven's sake, do not take those from me; let me have them to the last." They were returned to him.

'The next day at one o'clock he was taken to the place of execution, in a hackney coach at his own request. He conversed with ease and calmness with two Protestant clergymen who accompanied him, he being a Protestant, and, when he arrived at the gallows, seemed much disappointed at not being permitted to harangue the populace, giving reason to suppose that his intentions might fairly be trusted. But the experiment was one of too much danger; he was not allowed to speak, and finding he could not prevail, he calmly and at once advanced to the halter. He had before he left prison requested to have the Sacrament, and declared himself to live and to die a Christian, sincerely sorry for whatever he had done that was wrong, but dying in the firm persuasion that he had in the present instance acted up to what was his duty, according to every principle which from early infancy had been instilled into him.

'This request of partaking of the Sacrament (which was granted), but at the same time acknowledging no repentance for his conduct, produced a very warm dispute at his Excellency's table, where opinions were so equally divided that a Bishop being on the side *against* the administration of the Sacrament could scarce turn the scale. I will not venture upon a subject so far above me; but one thing I may venture to say, both with respect to Emmett and the two clergymen who administered, that I believe our great Creator, who looks into our hearts, will judge our motives rather than our actions. Our actions vary, as countries, habits, tenets of faith, and moral laws settle, but the motives of hearts are apart from religions and customs, and where they are sound and pure in their own tribunal—conscience— I do not believe that the great Judge of all will punish a person whose judgment only is wrong. Therefore, may we not forgive the clergymen, and perhaps, when we do, find an extenuation for Emmett?'[1]

The English again conquered the Cape in 1806. Lord Caledon went out as Governor, and Barnard

[1] Letter of Lady Anne Barnard to Viscount Melville, Dublin Castle, September 21, 1803.

was again appointed to his old post of Secretary to the Colony, it being thought that his knowledge of Cape affairs would prove useful. Lady Anne was very much against her husband accepting the appointment, but as nothing else offered he had perforce to go, and she arranged to follow him later. Her plans, however, were changed by the news of his death, which occurred soon after his arrival at the Cape, in 1807.

In her widowhood Lady Anne returned to Lady Margaret's house in Berkeley Square, where the sisters resided together, and she took up the thread of her life very much where it had been broken by her marriage. Among her best friends at this time were Sir Walter Scott and the Prince Regent. Some little time after Barnard's death Lady Anne sent a portrait of her husband to the Prince Regent with the following note:

'I know your goodness of heart, Sir, and I know that you will pardon this letter. It is not more to my prince that I write than to that kind friend and patron who would have stopped the fatal journey of my dear husband by an exchange of situation, had not untoward combinations defeated every hope and forced his departure. You will perceive, Sir, that it is Anne Barnard who now addresses your Royal Highness, to entreat your acceptance of what accompanies this. My dear husband requested in his will that I would send testimonies of his regard to those friends I knew he honoured and esteemed. To fulfil this desire, I have had an engraving done from this picture, of which the first proof is now sent to your Royal Highness. You will not be displeased at my venturing to place you, Sir, at the head of this (to me) sacred list—so much worth, and so many estimable qualities as he had, rendered him a person whose attachment could not disgrace even your Royal Highness. When you look at the print, Sir, as I hope you will do with regard for his sake, bestow a thought of pity and kindness on her who ever has been and must remain

'Your Royal Highness's

Most faithful and affectionate servant,

'ANNE BARNARD.

'P.S.—May I venture to say that I would rather your Royal Highness did not reply to my letter? Your heart will lead you to it, but it will be better for me not to receive any reply on this subject.'

The Prince Regent's reply shows that he possessed a warmth of heart with which many of his contemporaries did not credit him:

'My dear and old Friend,—You are right in thinking that perhaps it would be better, both for you and me, that no letter should pass between us in consequence of this recent mark of your kindest recollection and affection. But there are certain feelings which one is only individually responsible for, and that which perhaps in one instance is better for one person not to do, it is impossible for another to resist. It is not from any selfish conceit or presumption that I presume to differ from your much better reasoned and conceived opinion, but from the ingenuous and paramount impulse and feelings of a heart that you have long, long, long indeed known, which from the earliest hour of its existence has glowed with the warmest and most transcendent feelings of the most affectionate friendship for those who love and know how to appreciate it—and to whom can this be better applied, dearest Lady Anne, than to yourself? To tell you how much and how highly I value your present, and what (if it be possible) is much more, the affectionate remembrance you have shown me in this instance, and the manner in which you have done it, is that which I not only can never express, but can never forget. That every blessing and happiness may for ever attend you is the earnest prayer of

'Your ever and most affectionate friend,

'GEORGE P.

'P.S.—My heart is so full that I hope you will forgive this hasty scrawl, for I write the very instant I have received your letter. Pray tell me that you forgive me.'

Lady Margaret Fordyce married again in 1812 Sir James Burgess, and died two years later. Lady Anne continued to reside in Berkeley Square by herself, enjoying the esteem and society of her many friends. George IV. sent for her to come and see him when he was very ill. He spoke most affectionately to her, and said, 'Sister Anne' (the name he usually gave her), 'I wish to see you to tell you that I love you, and wish you to accept of this golden chain for my sake. I may, perhaps, never see you again.'

Lady Anne was always the life and soul of any party at which she was present. She was a great story-teller; the following is a characteristic illustration. She was entertaining a large party of distinguished guests at dinner when a hitch occurred in the kitchen. Her old servant came up behind her, and said, 'My Lady, you must tell another story—the second course won't be ready for five minutes.'

A few years before her death, Sir Walter Scott's novel 'The Pirate' appeared, in which book Sir Walter Scott who at that time refused to identify himself with the author of 'Waverley,' mentioned Lady Anne by name as the author of 'Auld Robin Gray.' He compared the condition of Minnie to that of Jeanie Gray—to quote his own words, 'The village heroine in Lady Anne Barnard's beautiful ballad.'[1] This public ascription led Lady Anne to think that the time had at last arrived to put an end to the disputes concerning the authorship of her ballad.

She wrote a letter to Sir Walter Scott, dated July 8, 1823, asking him to convey to the author of 'Waverley,' 'with whom,' she slyly added, 'I am informed you are personally acquainted, how grateful I feel the kindness with which he has, in the second volume of "The Pirate," chapter xiii., so distinguishedly noticed, and by his powerful authority assigned the long contested ballad of "Auld Robin Gray" to its proper author.' She then went on to say:

'In truth, the position I was placed in about that song had at last become irksome to me; how can I then so fully mark my thankfulness to him who has relieved me from my dilemma, as by transmitting to him, fairly and frankly, the origin, birth, life, death and confession, will and testament, of

[1] Nae langer she wept, her tears were a' spent,
Despair it was come and she thought it content;
She thought it content—but her cheek it grew pale
And she drooped like a snowdrop broke down by the hail.'

"Auld Robin Gray," with the assurance that the author of "Waverley" is the first person out of my own family who has ever had an explanation from me on the subject?

'"Robin Gray," so called from its being the name of the old herdsman at Balcarres, was *born* soon after the close of the year 1771. My sister Margaret had married and accompanied her husband to London; I was melancholy, and endeavoured to amuse myself by attempting a few poetical trifles. There was an ancient Scotch melody of which I was passionately fond; Sophy Johnstone, who lived before your day, used to sing it to us at Balcarres. I longed to sing old Sophy's air to different words, and to give to its plaintive tones some little history of virtuous distress in humble life, such as might suit it. While attempting to effect this in my closet, I called to my little sister, now Lady Hardwicke, who was the only person near me: "I have been writing a ballad, my dear. I am oppressing my heroine with many misfortunes: I have already sent her Jamie to sea, and broken her father's arm, and made her mother fall sick, and given her Auld Robin Gray for a lover, but I wish to load her with a fifth sorrow in the four lines, poor thing! Help me to one, I pray." "Steal the cow, sister Anne," said the little Elizabeth. The cow was immediately *lifted* by me, and the song completed. At our fireside, amongst our neighbours, "Auld Robin Gray" was always called for. I was pleased with the approbation it met with, but such was my dread of being suspected of writing anything, perceiving the shyness it created in those who could write nothing, that I carefully kept my own secret.'[1]

The last years of Lady Anne's life were spent in preparing and collecting materials for a book on the Lindsays. She died on May 6, 1825, in her seventy-fourth year. Her nephew, Colonel Lindsay, has paid the following tribute to her memory, which sums up the salient points in her remarkable and charming personality:

'The peculiar trait of Lady Anne's character was benevolence, a readiness to share with others her purse, her tears, or her joys—an absence of all selfishness. This, with her talents, created a power of pleasing which I have never seen equalled. She had in society a power of placing herself in sympathy with those whom she addressed, of drawing forth their feelings, their talents, their requirements, pleasing them with themselves, and consequently with their companions for the time being. I have often seen her change a dull party into an agreeable

[1] Letter of Lady Anne Barnard to Sir Walter Scott. Berkeley Square, London, July 8, 1823.

one; she could make the dullest speak, the shyest feel happy, and the witty flash fire without any apparent exertion. It were impossible to name the numbers who claimed her intimacy, even from the prince on the throne to the peasant at Balcarres.'

APPENDIX TO MEMOIR

THE ORIGINAL TEXT OF 'AULD ROBIN GRAY'

By LADY ANNE LINDSAY, by marriage BARNARD

When the sheep are in the fauld, when the kye's come hame,
And a' the weary warld to rest are gane,
The waes o' my heart fa' in showers frae my e'e,
Unkent by my gudeman, wha sleeps sound by me.

Young Jamie lo'ed me weel, and sought me for his bride,
But saving ae crown-piece he had naething beside;
To make the crown a pound my Jamie gaed to sea,
And the crown and the pound—they were baith for me.

He hadna been gane a twelvemonth and a day,
When my father brake his arm and the cow was stown away;
My mither she fell sick—my Jamie was at sea,
And Auld Robin Gray came a courting me.

My father couldna wark—my mither couldna spin—
I toiled day and night, but their bread I couldna win,—
Auld Rob maintained them baith, and, wi' tears in his e'e,
Said, 'Jeanie, O for their sakes will ye no marry me?'

My heart it said na, and I looked for Jamie back,
But hard blew the winds, and his ship was a wrack;
His ship was a wrack—why didna Jamie dee,
Or why am I spared to cry wae is me?

My father urged me sair—my mither didna speak,
But she looked in my face till my heart was like to break;
They gied him my hand—my heart was in the sea—
And so Robin Gray he was gudeman to me.

I hadna been his wife a week but only four,
When, mournfu' as I sat on the stane at my door,
I saw my Jamie's ghaist, for I couldna think it he
Till he said 'I'm come hame, love, to marry thee!'

Oh sair, sair did we greet, and mickle say of a',
I gied him ae kiss, and bade him gang awa',—
I wish that I were dead, but I'm na like to dee,
For though my heart is broken, I'm but young, wae is me!

I gang like a ghaist, and I carena much to spin,
I darena think o' Jamie, for that wad be a sin,
But I'll do my best a gude wife to be,
For, O, Robin Gray, he is kind to me.

LADY ANNE BARNARD'S LETTERS

I

As the following letters practically cover the period of the first British occupation of South Africa, a brief survey of the history of Cape Colony before it came into English hands may not be out of place.

The Cape of Good Hope was discovered by Bartholomew Dias, the Portuguese explorer, in 1486, when he was in search of an ocean road to India. His vessel was caught in a heavy gale, wherefore he entitled the new land 'Cabo Tormentoso,' or the Cape of Storms. The King of Portugal, appreciating the importance of the discovery, gave it the more auspicious name of the Cape of Good Hope, as its existence afforded a good hope of a new and easier way of reaching India, the goal of maritime expeditions of that age. The hope was realised ten years later, when Vasco da Gama doubled the Cape and carried the Portuguese flag into Indian seas. The Portuguese, more attracted by India, never valued the Cape at its proper worth; they often touched there, but they made no permanent settlement.

The ocean highway now being discovered, the English, Dutch, and French began to follow the

Portuguese to India *viâ* the Cape of Good Hope. The English flag was first seen in Table Bay in 1591. On the decline of the Portuguese power the Dutch established themselves in the East, and they early saw the importance of the Cape as a port of call and refreshment, it being regarded as two-thirds of the distance from Amsterdam to Batavia. They did not colonise it until 1652, when the Dutch East India Company ordered Jacob van Riebeck, with a small party of soldiers and colonists, to form a settlement there, something in the nature of a military outpost. These colonists gradually drove the Hottentots back and took their territory. The early settlers, though under Dutch rule, were not wholly Dutch, but were made up also of Flemings, Germans, Poles, and Portuguese, mostly of a low class. A few of the best, and those mainly Dutch, formed a Council to assist the chief officer in the management of the colony. In 1686 the little community received an important addition in a number of French refugees who had left their country on the revocation of the Edict of Nantes. This Huguenot immigration may still be traced in South Africa in many ways—Joubert and Du Plessis, for instance, are old Huguenot names. The colony now grew, gradually extending its borders and increasing its population. Cattle-breeding was found to pay, and became an important industry. The children and grandchildren of the Dutch, Germans, French, and other nationalities became *trek boeren*—that is, wandering farmers—and with their nomadic life they adopted unsettled and lawless habits.

For the next hundred years, throughout the eighteenth century, South Africa was under the rule, or rather the misrule, of the Dutch East India Company. They seized the territory of the Hottentots, broke their so-called contracts with them, and reduced those whom they did not kill to the position of serfs. They introduced a number of Malays and negroes into the colony as slaves—a measure absolutely indefensible, as there was no need of negro labour; they established a narrow and tyrannical policy, needlessly harassing the settlers with petty restrictions and extortionate taxes. They specified to the farmers the nature of the crops they were to grow, and exacted from them a large portion of their produce. This naturally led to false statements, bribery, cheating, and all kinds of corruption. Again and again were complaints made by the settlers to the Government in Holland against the Dutch East India Company, but without result. The Boers, or wandering farmers, were especially insubordinate, and not without reason; indeed, much of their dislike to orderly government may be traced back to this misgovernment. They made several attempts to throw off the rule of the Dutch East India Company, until at last, in 1795, their discontent culminated in active rebellion, and they endeavoured to form a republic of their own in the district of Graff-Reinet. At this time European politics had extended even to the Cape, and the French Revolution made its influence felt here, and found many sympathisers among the Dutch. In Holland there were two parties—the 'Patriot' party, which sympathised with the French and held republican principles; and the Orange party, which favoured the Stadtholders, the Prince of Orange, and the alliance with England. When war broke out the 'Patriot' party sided with France and the Orange party with the English. The French successes of 1794-5 had the result of upsetting the Prince of Orange's Government, and he escaped to England in a fishing-boat, and Holland, or that part of it in alliance with France, became known as the Batavian Republic.

Fearing that the Cape might fall into the hands of the French, and recognising its importance as a station on the way to India, the British Government resolved to take possession of it without delay. An expedition was despatched under Admiral Elphinstone and General Craig, who commanded the sea and land forces respectively, and arrived in Simon's Bay in June 1795. General Craig brought with him a letter from the Prince of Orange to the officers in charge at the Cape, desiring them to receive the English forces as in alliance with Holland. But the Cape officers, like the Dutch in Holland, were divided in their allegiance between the Patriot and the Orange factions, and they refused to recognise the mandate of a refugee prince, especially without instructions from their real masters, the Dutch East India Company. The English troops then landed under General Craig, and were reinforced shortly by 3,000 soldiers under General Sir Alured Clarke. After a short engagement the Dutch asked for an armistice, and the next day capitulated to the English, who took possession of the castle and the garrison of the Cape of Good Hope, and hoisted the British flag. Thus ended the rule of the Dutch East India Company in South Africa.

After the capitulation, the civil government and military command of the Cape were placed in the hands of General Craig, who became the temporary head of the English Government there. His brief rule was judicious and conciliatory; he interfered as little as possible with the existing state of things, and was respected by the Dutch. Soon after the news of the conquest of the Cape reached England the Government resolved to appoint Lord Macartney as Governor, and to vest in him all the power held by the Governor and Council of the Dutch East India Company. They also determined to greatly increase the garrison at Cape Town, and to make the officer in command the Lieutenant-Governor. General Francis Dundas, nephew of the Secretary of State, was given this post, and Mr. Barnard was appointed Secretary to the Colony. In all these appointments the influence of Lord Melville may be clearly traced. The King rewarded General Craig with a K.C.B. for his services, and the decoration was taken out by the new Governor, Lord Macartney, who, with the Secretary of the Colony and Lady Anne Barnard, arrived at Cape Town in May 1797, and took over the duties of government. At this point Lady Anne's letters begin.

II

The Castle, Cape Town :
July 10th, 1797.

FROM the Castle of Good Hope, situated within the garrison, over which towers the Table Mountain at a considerable real distance (the close apparent vicinity being from the effect of its height), and from the window of my bed-chamber, which overlooks a colonnade built around a spacious pond of water supplied from the head and tail of a spouting dolphin, I begin this letter to my dearest Friend,[1] firmly assured that he will be as much interested in its contents from private affection to the writer, as from curiosity to know every point, however minute, which regards a public concern. I am perfectly convinced that you must also receive along with this such numberless letters from others much better qualified to give you an account of everything worth your knowing, that it would seem almost conceited folly in me to describe things as they appear around me, or still more to give my miserable female notions on anything of importance, were it not that I know your friendship will contrive a general apology for

[1] The Right Hon. Henry Dundas, Secretary of State, to whom all these letters are addressed.

everything silly or erroneous, and though all seems yellow to the jaundiced eye, all will seem rose colour and interesting to that partial pair of black sparklers with which you read the epistles of your female friend. You gave me leave to write freely whenever I would, and I promise that you shall find everything you wish to know—and some things you may not—from the honestest pen in the world (for I must not confine myself now to Europe). I never exaggerate —never; sometimes I may extenuate, but I set down naught in malice.

But to land us here properly, let me first return to the ship and bring up matter with a little regularity.

Our voyage on the whole was a prosperous one. We sailed from Plymouth the 23rd of February, and landed at the Cape the 5th of May. We had but few calms, and no storm such as to endanger the ship, though ten days of weather was so very rough as to give sufficient apology to a coward for being afraid, particularly from the rolling of the ship. We had, as you know, 272 great guns for Bengal aboard her, which often brought our upper guns under water, and rendered the beauties in their various cabins black and blue from the rolling and pitching the guns produced. We met with but few occurrences of consequence. The heat between the Tropics was excessive, but not beyond or equal to what I expected, as the thermometer was never above 84 degrees. We passed the Line exactly at twelve o'clock, the Sun in his

Meridian, and on his way from his country seat of Capricorn to that of Cancer. I made a few little drawings of sharks, dolphins, flying fish, hardly worth your looking at, which I shall send to Margaret,[1] the only merit of which consists in their being literally just. All on board were well, partly owing to the dry weather, partly to the attentions of the Captain, who you very justly told me was one of the civilest and most liberal of men. Our messmates numbered about twenty-four, and we all got on like lambs, except two, of whom I would say nothing, were it not that you must hear of them from others. I mean Captain Campbell and his Dutch wife. We were obliged to drop common conversation with them beyond the necessities of society. He contradicted all around him in a manner most unusual in civilised company, and as for Mrs. Campbell, after every fair attention on the part of the ladies on board, who were five beside herself, she seemed resolved to keep herself apart from all *Englishwomen*, apparently reserving herself to be head of the Dutch party instead of the English, and finding much fault with Government for sending to the Cape, as she says, a 'parcel of people who cannot please the Dutch, or be likely to adopt their manners.' I hope that her manners are not a specimen, and that her calculations will not prove good, as the Dutch are said to be eager to be well with the English. In any case Mr. Barnard

[1] Her sister, Lady Margaret Fordyce.

and I mean to do all in our power to carry out your wishes, to conciliate them as much as we possibly can, and to meet their habits and the custom of the place half-way.

But to return to our voyage. The heat decreased as we passed the Tropic of Cancer, and, after having quitted our blankets and cloth habits, we all took to them again. Our course was pretty direct by the chart from the time we passed the Madeiras (where you made us go into a fine scollop to avoid certain French cruisers which we have since heard you had intelligence of) till we got into the latitude of the Cape, where contrary winds vexed us much, and blew us very nearly into the latitude where the 'Guardian' was lost by mountains of ice. However, five or six days produced a favourable change, and the joyful news of land being seen was announced, though in truth it was so enveloped in fog that we did not enjoy its appearance till we were exactly placed in the bay opposite to Cape Town. Then, as if by one consent, the Lion's rump whisked off the vapours with its tail; the Lion's head untied, and dropped the necklace of clouds which surrounded its erect throat, and Table Mountain, over which a white damask table-cloth had been spread half-way down, showed its broad face and smiled. At the same time guns from the garrison and from all the batteries welcomed His Majesty's Government, and the distant hills, who could not step forward to declare their allegiance, by the awful thunders of their acquiescing echoes, informed us that they were not ignorant of the arrival of the Governor,[1] who was at that moment putting his foot on land. Nothing could be finer than the *coup d'œil* from the Bay; yet nothing can have so little affinity with each other as the bold perpendicular mountains, bare and rocky, and the low white card houses, which from the distance seem even smaller than they are, and scarce large enough to hold an ant. But this is only appearance, in reality they are excellent.[2]

The Thornborns, having heard of our arrival, sent us an invitation to come to their house, which was a blessing of no moderate sort, every place being crowded. Lord Macartney preferred going to one of the lodging-houses (indeed all the private houses, half a dozen excepted, are such) to incommoding Sir James Craig[3] by going to his abode. We walked from the Key to Mr. Thornborn's house, for though his carriage was sent to meet us, we preferred the

[1] George, Earl Macartney, the first English Governor of the Cape of Good Hope, had enjoyed a distinguished career as a diplomatist and Colonial Governor. He had been Envoy Extraordinary to the Court of St. Petersburg, and concluded a most successful commercial treaty with Russia; he had been Governor of Madras, and had refused the Governor-Generalship of India. He had been on a special embassy to the Emperor of China at Pekin. He was appointed Governor of the Cape of Good Hope on December 30, 1796, and arrived there on board the 'Trusty,' May 4, 1797.

[2] The population of Cape Town was then about 6,000 Europeans and nearly 11,000 persons of colour.

[3] General Sir James Henry Craig had assumed the civil government and military command at the Cape after the capitulation of the Dutch, and remained there as Deputy-Governor of the colony until the arrival of Lord Macartney.

feeling of hard land under our feet to all artificial conveyances. The first thing that struck me, strongly and disagreeably, was a very offensive smell in the air, and I afterwards found it in some of the houses; I was told it proceeded from the oil with which the slaves grease their hair. Waggons of wood next appeared, driven by one man, eight and ten horses moving with perfect docility to the crack of his whip. Next we saw more melancholy evidences of the far distant classes amongst human creatures— slaves returning from a seven or eight miles' distance, each man loaded with two bundles of sticks slung across his bare shoulders. It made one sigh at first in looking at the weight of the bundles; the only comfort was that one of them only was for the master, the other was for the private benefit of the slave. We walked up the town, which I found much superior in appearance and area, and in the size and accommodation of the houses, to what I had expected. We were kindly welcomed by the Thornborns, who let us make their house our home during ten days and, much unlike the Dutch system, would accept of no repayment. But she is an Englishwoman, he is a Dane, and both are the intimate friends of our sweet Doctor Gillan,[1] who I hope is at this moment as well as we wish him.

Long looked-for as Lord Macartney had been, his arrival seemed to give new life to languid spirits.

[1] A well-known Scottish physician who had accompanied Lord Macartney on his special mission to China in 1793.

Even the Dutch, who had vainly flattered themselves till a Governor came that a Governor never would come, and that the Cape would somehow or another fall back into the old hands[1] or be ceded to the French, seemed to have got a cold bath first, but revived health and alacrity of mind through certainty of the worst, and the necessity of beginning business again on an assured footing. This has not been the case during the procrastinated decisions of Sir James Craig, who has made it his policy to delay all unpleasant rules until the commencement of the new Governor's administration. I fancy that on the capture of the Cape, being too eager to obtain it, he made the terms of capitulation unnecessarily beneficial to the Dutch. He wished to be the friend and protector of the Cape people, and so unwittingly made himself the protector of Dutch impositions put upon the troops—a dear price for popularity. He considered these indulgences were merely temporary ones, as a Governor would soon arrive. Meantime, through his eagerness to conciliate and to keep well with the Dutch inhabitants of the Colony, we found that every article of life had been permitted to rise to an immoderate price, unchecked by any scheme of abatement by competition, or by prevailing on the farmers to bring down their stock, and that there was an actual scarcity of grain in the place. The number of mouths to be fed was now three times as many, while that granary which the Dutch policy

[1] The Dutch East India Company.

had always kept filled with one or two years' grain beforehand, and which would now have stood us in good stead, had loaded a few ships, to be a breakfast for London and to prove the abundance of the Colony. Bread of course was raised, but not very essentially, as grain is ground all through, and brown bread of a coarser quality than what you have usually seen (of which I send you a bit), but I think good, is universally used, much to the annoyance of the Dutch, who reckon themselves undone if they are without the finest. They, however, sustain but little of this inconvenience, as they are too provident not to have a private stock of everything, which is kept up till an opportunity be found of selling to advantage; nor is there one house in Cape Town where any article may not be bought in a clandestine manner if a tempting price is paid. But the master pretends to know nothing of the matter, as there is a great degree of false pride amongst them, no one choosing to confess he does the things which all do, and all know are done.

Immediately on our arrival, Mr. Thornborn's house was filled with scarlet and blue coats, who came to visit us and to rejoice on our arrival. I should have felt sorry, when I listened to the dislike every individual expressed of the Cape without reserve, had I not hoped that many favourable changes would soon take place from Lord Macartney's wisdom, and from the acquisition society was gaining by a few good-humoured people being thrown into the leaven tub, which at that moment appeared to have too much acid in it. I plainly saw from General Craig's manner that he was disappointed at not remaining here himself, but, since he was not to do so, it was very agreeable to him to go to India. He appeared, however, to be much less sanguine in his expectations of the benefits arising to England from the Cape, or from the possibility of its being rendered flourishing, convenient, or any *real acquisition* to us, than I had imagined he would have been. He boldly said that the expectations formed from it, and of it, were too high. One could only pause and listen to this with a portion of regret, mixed with another little portion of distrust of a judgment which, though a very tolerable one in many respects, is not so extensive in its views or powers as some others I wot of. Admiral Pringle,[1] however, backed this gloomy view with six-and-thirty-pounder corroborations. He said that the Cape was the worst nautical situation it was possible for the devil himself to contrive, with fewer possibilities of harbourings or landing-places than could be conceived—no rivers, no water, torrents in plenty from the mountain tops, but nothing in the bosom of the earth. He imagined also that the Dutch policy was a sound one when they checked all population or improvement, for as the Colony improved and peopled he thought it would to *us* only prove a

[1] The Admiral then commanding the squadron at the Cape.

second America, and would be more likely in time to rob us of India than to secure it for us. He held all establishment of manufactures to be dangerous and foolish, and said that no pains should be taken with the interior of the country, but merely with the skirting of it, which could produce comforts to our people after their long voyages to and fro. All this the Admiral laid down much more clearly, God knows, than I repeat it; and he wound up by swearing that the Cape was the 'cussedest place' ever discovered, with nothing good in it, and that even the hens did not lay fresh eggs, so vile was every animal that inhabited the place.

There appeared to be no small mixture of prejudice, along with some reasonable causes of dislike, in all these explosions. I could only cry pause here also, and wait to hear the other side of the question; but this I was not likely to have from the military, who all to a man have disliked their quarters—nor is that much to be wondered at, as everything since the first capture of the Cape has been so extravagantly dear that the poor subalterns are both starved and undone. The private soldiers live well, and cheap, as beef, mutton, and bread are still reasonable, the first being only $2\frac{1}{2}d.$ per pound, raised to $4d.$ per pound now; and I suppose bread is not more, or so much, as in London, as our house bills for it amount to nearly the same sum as it cost us there. At first there was much drinking amongst the private soldiers, from the cheapness of the Cape wine, which could then be procured for about 3d. a bottle ; but now I have heard there are wine-taxes laid on it, or some way is contrived to render its attainment less easy and counteract its pernicious effects in the garrison, it being now 6d. a bottle, or more. Every other article of life (the three excepted—wine, bread, and butcher's meat) is extraordinarily dear. An officer, who comforts himself on going to this distant destination by the thought of living within his pay, is therefore disappointed in the extreme to find that he is obliged to spend more here than if he were in London. This is by no means owing to his purchasing English articles, as the products of the country are equally expensive—garden-stuff, fruit, eggs, butter, washing, labour, all are above all reason : an egg is 3d., a pound of potatoes 6d., a dish of cauliflower 1s. 6d., milk above 1s. per quart, the washing of a shirt 6d., oranges about the same price as in London, almonds, raisins, walnuts nearly the same, and every assistance of labour three times as much. All this, together with the high price of horses (an ordinary one being 30l. or 40l.), with fodder enormous and not to be obtained, besides the want of amusement of every kind, has made the military sick of this place, vexed as they have been with scarcity and poverty, and hipped with *ennui*. Perhaps their distance from the fountain of *promotion* may add to this, and the very little notice taken of the subaltern officers (which has come to a point Mr. Barnard and I think very cruel, and wish to mend as far as we can) has rendered them still more dispirited; no man here beneath a colonel, or major at least, being invited to anything.

I soon had an opportunity of judging of this. Sir James Craig gave a ball to the new Governor in honour of his arrival, to which we, of course, went. I must say it was a very pretty sight: the Government House in the gardens was beautifully lighted with every lamp in the Colony which could be brought together, and the walks, shadowed with oak trees, were bright as day, and had very pretty devices at the end of most of them. The ball-room was very long but somewhat narrow; perhaps it seemed narrow because it was lined with rows of Dutch ladies, all tolerably well-dressed, much white muslin about, and a good deal of colour. I had been told that the Dutch ladies were handsome as to their faces, but I saw no real beauty, though they were fresh and wholesome-looking; while as for manner, they had none, and graces and charms were sadly lacking, though they had a sort of vulgar smartness, which I suppose passed for wit. They danced without halting at all, a sort of pit-a-pat little step, which they have probably learned from some Beauty on her way to Bengal. They remind me very much of the women one might find at an assize ball in a country town. What they want most is shoulders and manners. I know now what is meant by a 'Dutch doll'; their make is exactly like them. But the most exceptional things about them are their teeth and the size of their feet. A tradesman in London, hearing their feet were so large, sent a box of shoes on speculation, which almost put the Colony in a blaze, so angry were the Beauties. But day by day a pair was sent for by a slave in the dark, until at last all the shoes vanished. But I think that these people will improve on acquaintance, and have only to be more understood; for my part, I am resolved to be pleased with everything. I was, at the ball, all smiles, as honesty here would be by no means the best policy. There were not many Dutchmen there; the Fiscal,[1] or head officer of Justice, the President of the Court, and one or two other men in public positions, appeared for a short time and then vanished, as if they were almost afraid of being seen there by each other. They cannot divest themselves of the opinion that the English will be obliged to cede the Cape to the Dutch, or to France, on a peace, and therefore do not want to get known as partisans of the English Government. As for the young Dutchmen, I saw hardly any; the young ones prefer smoking their pipes on the *stoep*, or perhaps they are altogether Jacobin. At any rate they were not there, and this brings me back to the point where I started.

[1] Willem Stephanus van Ryneveld, who had held the same office under the Dutch East India Company.

I was surprised to see so small a portion of the military; no ensigns, lieutenants, or their wives. I asked about this, and found out that it is the *ton* of the general officers to discountenance the subordinate ranks from mixing in society. I think this is very bad for the young military, and I have heard that— for want of a better society, we shall suppose it—the garrison were much given to drinking and gaming. Every day this prevails less and less. General Dundas[1] does not encourage either—indeed, in my opinion, considerably the contrary. At review-dinners, and on such public festivities, he pushes about the bottle in a manly way; but except on these occasions never, and gaming he never gives in to. You would be pleased to see how wisely, temperately, and agreeably he conducts himself in his situation, how well he and Lord Macartney are together, and on what comfortable terms he is with all around him. I dwell the more on this, as there was a time when I remember hearing him called hot and haughty; if such things have been, or are, in his temper, they are at present checked and laid aside; he is a most pleasant member of society, and well liked by man and woman. I see also great satisfaction in every one with the manners of our Lord, who was expected to be cold and dignified, and fond of his own opinion,

[1] General Francis Dundas, second son of Robert Dundas of Arniston, and nephew of the Right Hon. Henry Dundas (afterwards Viscount Melville), was appointed to command the troops at the Cape of Good Hope in August 1796. He was also Lieutenant-Governor, and afterwards Acting-Governor on two occasions.

and stiff in maintaining it. Such was the public notion of him: he certainly has wished to impress it differently, and has succeeded. He promotes society, and is markedly attentive to the individuals who compose it, respects those inferior to himself in their departments, lays down rules with wise firmness but no mixture of pride, and is (I may say), as far as things have come, beloved. I shall only quote you the words of one smallish man, as it contains more than his own feelings. 'I am so glad,' said he, 'to find myself a gentleman now. I had begun to fancy myself a blackguard, but I look up to myself now from the manner Lord Macartney treats me.'

Lord Macartney, immediately on his arrival, declared his intention of living in the Government House in the garden, which he apprehended would not be too cold in winter, and which is certainly cooler than any other here in summer. General Dundas was the next to make his election; he preferred remaining in the second-sized house within the Castle—being fixed there with a proper bachelor establishment—to occupying the great Government House, which required more furniture and servants, and was fitter for a family. This he gave up to us, partly from good-humour and partly from the above reasons. It is a palace, containing such a suite of apartments as makes me fancy myself a princess when in it—but not an Indian or Hottentot princess, as I have fitted all up in the style of a comfortable, plain, English house. Scotch carpets,

English linen, and rush-bottom chairs, with plenty of lolling sofas, which I have had made by regimental carpenters and stuffed by regimental tailors. In a week or two I shall invite all who wish to be merry without cards or dice, but who can talk, or *hop* to half a dozen black fiddlers, to come and see me on my public day, which shall be once a fortnight, when the Dutch ladies (all of whom love dancing, and flirting still more) shall be kindly welcomed, and the poor ensigns and cornets shall have an opportunity of stretching their legs as well as the generals. I shall not be stinted for room, as I have a hall of sixty feet, a drawing-room of forty, a dining-room of twenty, a tea-room of thirty, and three supper-rooms—in one of which only I shall have supper, and that cold and desultory, with side-boards and no chairs, as I wish to make my guests happy without being ruined by their drinking half a hogshead of claret every party. Ducks and chickens, etc., they shall have, but as turkeys are one pound apiece, I shall not fly at any of their excellencies.

At Rondebosch is the pleasantest country house belonging to Government, four miles distance from the Cape; it has been occupied by General Campbell—Lord Macartney begged him and his wife to remain in it, which they have done. I like our house in the garrison better, however, than any we could have had elsewhere, as it is close by the office, where Mr. Barnard is from ten in the morning to three or four, and sometimes part of the evening.

I ought perhaps to leave it to Lord Macartney to say how he is pleased with the Secretary; but to *You* I cannot resist expressing the great satisfaction I feel in seeing Mr. Barnard get through the business of his situation in a manner which I perceive is completely satisfactory to Lord Macartney, and so conciliatory to every one around him. I always knew that his abilities would be found equal to any demand that could be made on them, but I feel this conjecture established into a very pleasant certainty by having, on more occasions than one, seen Lord Macartney throwing on him very consequential decisions which have been invariably approved of, and even adopting from time to time alterations which Mr. Barnard has ventured to make in papers after Lord Macartney has approved of them. Lord Macartney, on the other hand, seems positively fond of, and most companionable with, Mr. Barnard, who appears, and is, as happy in his department as a man can be who thirsted after employment, had it bestowed on him by a friend he is glad to be obliged to, and feels himself equal to it.

With such reasons for being happy, if I tell you that *I* am happy, and I like the Cape, and see much of the disgust with which it is talked of by others as arising out of their own acrid humours, but half-supported by the fact, you will not be surprised. You must, however, read my account of its merits, when I begin to expatiate on them, with some grains of allowance, as well as those opinions against on the other side, as I know that I have a natural disposition to pick out flowers amongst weeds if I can, and to make the best of all ' existing circumstances.' But, independent of this being the turn of my mind, let us look at the facts. Here is a divine climate (at least I have found it so as yet), no fog, no damp, no variations to check the perspirations and fall on the lungs, but a clear, pure, yet not sharp air, full of health and exhilaration to the spirits. Here *is* scarcity, but here will be plenty, I am convinced, when the harvest comes round, which quickly follows the sowing here—at least a third quicker than in England. The farmers saw no certain market before for their grain, nor would they venture to sow what was in their granaries, for fear of its being reaped by they knew not whom. Now that there is a fixed government and a certain allowance for all, they can send down to the shore. Less will probably be raised this year than will be necessary to make things very cheap, but industry will be doubled next year, more slaves will be got, more cattle taken into the yoke, and plenty, I think, will ensue. The town is clean, one or two dirty circumstances attending the killing of animals excepted; the features upon Nature's face magnificently strong. I love these bold strokes with which the Almighty has separated the dry land from sea in His chaos. The bay opens beautifully at the foot of the mountains, while the Hottentot hills at twenty miles' distance rise in forms so stupendously eccentric

that I look at them with admiration every time I
see them. It is in the power of activity and taste
to make this, by planting, the finest scene in the
world. I have but little of either, but little as I
have, if I was only sure of living a couple of hundred
years, to see the effects of my labours, I would begin
to plant to-morrow with alacrity those grounds
round the town which, from their want of water,
cannot be applied to any purpose save that of rear-
ing wood, which I think they could do in plenty for
the use of the town : the silver tree and Scotch fir
particularly growing to perfection, 'and join the
gentle to the rude.' The marriage of Miss Silver-
tree with Donald Fir-tops is exactly what I quote,
the lady being covered with leaves of grey satin,
and the fir, stout, of a fresh bold green, and hardy
as its countrymen. I hear you say, and you speak it
like a great man, like a good man, like a man of a
mind far more extensive than any country is, ' But
why must you live to two hundred years to plant ?
Can't you plant though you should live only twenty
years ?—some one in future will have the benefit of
it and thank you.' I can, to be sure—and I will,
that is more. I will do as much as my private purse
can fairly do for public spirit, but a great deal I
can't, unless I can persuade others to do so too, as
the ground so planted must be enclosed, else the
little tender sticks would be torn up by the slaves
for firewood in a twelvemonth's time.

There is a plan (I am not sure by whom

suggested) of making a sort of navigable canal or connection by water, and by the Burgh river between the sea at False Bay (or Simon's Bay as they call it here), to fall into the salt river at the foot of the Table Mountain. If this could be done it would be a great thing for this place. The expense was talked of as great, but, Lord bless me! if we keep the Cape, John Bull would fill the subscription of 200,000*l*. in the course of a morning on 'Change.

But I must have done, or you'll think I'll never stop. Adieu, my dearest friend. My love to dear Lady Jane. Tell her to think of me sometimes in this land of ostriches, Kaffirs, and Hottentots. God bless you all.

III

The Castle, Cape of Good Hope:
August 10th, 1797.

I MUST begin my letter, my dear Friend, by telling you of the steps which have been taken to bring the people of the Cape into harmony with our English Government. There was a Proclamation to the effect that during a certain time, which was an ample one, they might come from all quarters and take the oath of allegiance to His Majesty. The gates of the Castle were thrown open every morning, and I was surprised to see so many come after what I had heard. Firstly came a number of well-fed, rosy-cheeked men, with powdered hair, and dressed in black. They walked in in pairs with their hats off, a regulation on entering the Castle on public occasions which, in former days, Dutch pride imposed. They were followed by the Boers from the country—farmers and settlers who had come some very great distance. I think that many of them seemed very sulky and ill-affected; their manner seemed to say: 'There is no help for it. We must swear, for they are the strongest.' They are very fine men, their height is enormous; most of them are six feet high and upwards, and I do not know how many feet across; I hear that five or six hundred miles distant they even reach seven feet. They all came to the Cape in waggons, bringing a load of something to market at the same time. They were dressed in blue cloth jackets and trousers and very high flat hats. In fact, they struck me as overdressed, but the Hottentot servant who crept behind each, carrying his master's umbrella, on the other hand, was underdressed. He seemed to have little else to carry except a piece of leather round his waist and a sheepskin round his shoulders; one or two had a scarlet handkerchief tied round the head, sometimes an old hat ornamented with ostrich feathers, but very often they were bareheaded. I was told the Hottentots were uncommonly ugly and disgusting, but I do not think them so bad. Their features are small and their cheek-bones immense, but they have a kind expression of countenance; they are not so ugly as the slaves of Mozambique. I must try to sketch a face of every caste or nation here; the collection cannot be short of twenty.

I must now tell you a little about a Cape expedition of mine. Having been told that no woman had ever been on the top of the Table Mountain (this was not literally true, one or two having been there), and being unable to get any account of it from the inhabitants of this town, all of whom wished it to be considered as next to an impossible matter to get to the top of it, as an excuse for their own want of curiosity, and having found the officers all willing to believe the Dutch for ditto reason, laziness to wit, there was some ambition as a motive for climbing, as well as curiosity. And as Mr. Barrow [1] is just one of the pleasantest, best-informed, and most eager-minded young men in the world about everything curious or worth attention, I paid him my addresses and persuaded him to mount the mountain along with me. We were joined in the plan by two of my ship-mates, officers, and my maid chose to be of the party. I had a couple of servants, and a couple of boxes with cold meat and wine. Mr. Barrow and I slung round our shoulders tin cases for plants, of which we were told we should get great variety on the top of the mountain. It is 3,500 feet in height, and reckoned about three miles to the top of it from the beginning of the great ascent, the road being (or rather the conjectured path, for there is no road) necessarily squinted in the zigzag way which much increases the measurement of the walk. At eight o'clock in the morning Mr. Barrow and I, with our followers, set off. We reached the foot of the mountain on horseback, and dismounted when we could ride no more—indeed, nothing but a human creature or an antelope could ascend such a path.

We first had to scramble up the side of a pretty perpendicular cascade of a hundred feet or two, the

---

[1] Mr., afterwards Sir Henry, Barrow was a naturalist and explorer, and one of Lord Macartney's private secretaries. He was employed by Lord Macartney to examine into the natural resources of the Colony, and explore the almost unknown territory to the north of it. He later became Auditor-General, with a salary of 1,000*l*. a year.

falls of which must be very fine after rains, and the sides of which were shaded with myrtles, sugar trees, and geraniums. We continued our progress through a low foliage of all sorts of pretty heaths and evergreens, the sun at last beginning to beat with much force down on our heads, but the heat was not, though great, oppressive. Wherever we saw questionable stone or ore, Mr. Barrow attacked it with a hammer, which I had luckily brought for the purpose, but he found the mountain through all its strata, of which there are innumerable, composed of *iron stone*, and that at least to the quantity of fifty per cent. It made me smile to see the signs of human footsteps, in the quantity of old soles and heels of shoes which I came across every here and there. I suppose these relics have lain time immemorial, as leather, I believe, never decays, at least not for a great while. They proved that the Dutchmen told fibs when they said that few people had tried to get up this mountain. The sun and fatigue obliged me frequently to sit down; and as I had an umbrella with me, a few minutes always recruited me. At last, about twelve o'clock, the sun began to be so very hot that I rejoiced at the turn of the mountain, which I saw would soon bring us into the shadow, before we reached the great gully by which we were to get out on the top. Redoubling my activity, at last we made the turn, but it was wonderful the sudden chill which instantaneously came over us; we looked at our thermometers, and in a second they had fallen under the shadow fifteen degrees, being now 55, and before, on the brow of the hill, they were 70. We had now come to a fine spring of water, which fell from the top of the rock, or near it, over our heads; we drank some of it with port-wine, but it was too cold to have been safe, if we had not more way to climb. I saved a bottle of it for you, *cher ami*. Opposite there was a cave cut in the rock, which is occasionally inhabited by runaway negroes, of which there were traces.

Once more we set off, and in three hours from the bottom of the mountain reached the very tip-top of this great rock, looking down on the town (almost out of sight below) with much conscious superiority, and smiling at the formal meanness of its appearance, which would have led us to suppose it built by children out of half a dozen packs of cards. I was glad on this pinnacle to have a bird's-eye view of the country, the bays, and the distant and near mountains. The *coup d'œil* brought to my awed remembrance the Saviour of the World presented from the top of 'an exceeding high mountain' with all the kingdoms of the earth by the devil. Nothing short of such a view was this. But it was not the garden of the world that appeared all around; on the contrary, there was no denying the circle bounded only by the heavens and sea to be a wide desert, bare, uncultivated, uninhabited, but noble in its bareness, and (as we had reason to know) possessing a soil capable of cultivation, a soil, which submits easily to the spade, and gratefully repays attention. On the top of the mountain there was nothing of that luxuriancy of verdure and foliage, flower or herbage, described by travellers; there were roots and some flowers, and a beautiful heath on the edge of the rocks, but the soil was cold, swampy, and mossy, covered in general with half an inch of water, rushes growing in it, and sprinkled all over with little white pebbles, some dozens of which I gathered to make Table Mountain earrings for my fair European friends. We now produced our cold meat, our port, Madeira, and Cape wine, and we made a splendid and happy dinner after our fatigues. When it was over I proposed a song to be sung in full chorus, not doubting that all the hills around would join us— 'God save the King.'[1] 'God save great George our King,' roared I and my troop. 'God save—God save—God save—God save—God save—God save— God save—God save—great George our King—great George our King—great George—great George— great George—' repeated the loyal mountains. 'The impression is very fine,' said Mr. Barrow, with his eyes glistening. I could not say 'Yes,' because I felt more than I chose to trust my voice with, just then, but I wished 'great George our King' to have stood beside me at the moment, and to have thrown his eye over his new colony, which we were thus (his humble viceroys) taking possession of in his name.

King George III.

My servants shot a few pretty birds, which you shall see by-and-by, and we found it time to return home, which we could not reach, we saw, before six o'clock at night. Nothing was more singular than to look down far, far below, on the flag raised on the top of the Lion's head, a rock perpendicular, of some hundred feet, on the top of a great North Berwick law. It is round this rock that there is a constant necklace of clouds playing; but on this day all was clear. The person who keeps guard on this rock is drawn up by ropes fixed in a particular manner.

If it was difficult to ascend the hill, it was much more so to descend. The ladies were dressed for the occasion, else—I need not say more after the word 'else.' The only way to get down was to sit down and slip from rock to rock the best way one could. My shoes I had tied on with some yards of tape, which had been a good scheme. At last we reached home, not more tired than I expected we should have been, and more than ever convinced that there are few things impossible where there is, in man or woman, a decided and spirited wish of attainment. Doctor Pattison (a very amiable, sensible, and humane man sent out by the Admiralty as physician to the Navy Hospital) told me there was no sum he could not have won at the Cape against my ever reaching the top of Table Mountain. He said he would not take them in, for he knew I would do it if it was possible for anybody to do it, as I had said

I would. I had found, however, no further gratification from having been there than the pleasure of being able to say, 'I have seen it,' for my fancy could have painted the same very prettily, without going up.

Since that time I have ridden round the Bay; the road is finer than any scene I ever saw in my life, or could have seen—that is to say, fine from mountains and sea. I must make some sketches of this road, but my time has been as yet wholly occupied with domestic cares. I am a Martha, with the full intention of being twenty better things by-and-by; meantime, as we have a great many people who eat and drink with us in a family way, and as it is extremely difficult to get many things, or servants to do them properly, I am obliged to be more of a useful than an accomplished female; but if I can in any way make things comfortable to my kind husband and his friends I am well employed. I see a great deal of your friends the Campbells—I mean the General and his wife. She is a good-humoured, pleasant, good-looking creature with a very good heart, and is much calculated to render society pleasant and easy. The General you know to be a respectable and gentleman-like man. Of the other Campbells I cannot say so much. In my former letter I mentioned how much they had endeavoured to make themselves disagreeable in their various ways on board ship; I had really been afraid from what General Hartley said (and from her own manners) that she would endeavour to set up a Dutch party against the Englishwomen going out; but I am glad to find that nothing is in her power. She is very much disliked here, even by her countrywomen, and he equally so, nor would she be at all in the foreground of society was she not tempted (which I will suppose is by a love of receiving notice) to go rather too great lengths with most of the gentlemen to obtain it. Her character has not yet had time to be very naughty, but with three or four flirtations going on at present it is rather equivocal. Amongst the Dutch women this is nothing—each one has her lover, and, if more, it only the more proves her charms. I have blushed to hear one of her sisters make her child count up 'Mama's sweethearts' on its little fingers, when some of the sweethearts present knew it to be no joke, as some others in England could have corroborated. Captain Campbell was very haughty at first to everybody, but I believe he has been taken down some pegs by Admiral Pringle. We had them to dine here lately—we wish to have *no* quarrels and no miffs. They had wished to miff with us, but we are so civil, without familiarity, that they cannot make it out, so now they eat our mutton, and gulp.

Amongst a few gentlemen who augur more good from the Cape than others is Mr. Thornborn—he thinks highly of its powers and fertility. Mr. Barrow also is of this party; both of these, however, think that *this* is not the best situation for the Capital, but that Simon's Bay would have been better, had it water, and water I dare say might be found if dug for skilfully. I wish the King would send out his friend Lady Millbank with her hazel wand—she would poke up and down till she found plenty, and we should have a second 'Judith's well,' as at the Duke of Manchester's. It is thought that hemp might be raised here with benefit to our mother country and with success. There is no barley here—that is a grain which should also be brought. Beef is certainly inferior to what it is in England, and so is mutton, which is not thought of on t'other side of the water. The fat of the first is too yellow, and of the last too white, but neither is at present well fed. The sheep's tails are very useful for anything lard would be used for, as they are much purer than lard, and far better than the butter here. At first one has a prejudice against them, but now I have them used and say nothing. Poultry is about as good as in England, but milk and butter inferior, and the Cape cows good for nothing; the half-breed along with the English ones are better, and sell very high. I had an English cow, but she is no more—she died of rheumatism and a liver complaint. I had no good fare for her, poor cow, and a long walk every day to pick up her grass did not agree with her.

I hope soon to have poultry and vegetables of our own, as there is a little Government cottage at the bottom of the mountain, called 'Paradise,' which Lord Macartney has given us to be rural in. It has not enough of ground uncleared to have a cow, but it will at least raise us chickens and potatoes. There is no road to it—or rather a road practicable only on horseback—but as it is only a place to hide our heads in the shade when the sun gets sultry, we don't much care about that. The roof is thatched and old, admitting the rain, which rots the timbers; but a new roof of reeds, which the place will furnish, will not cost much. There is a little hasty stream of water, a clump of firs, a good many old orchard trees, a few orange trees, a perpendicular rock behind, and a far extended view of mountains and sea before, the intermediate space being uncultivated heath or short stubbed wood, good for little but the oven. Of a Saturday John and Joan and Jane the cousin will 'noddy' it down, leaving the carriage at the bottom of the hill to walk up it, and will there hide themselves till Monday, visited only by a few monkeys from the mountains, perhaps a wolf, possibly some runaway negroes, but all these (the monkeys excepted, who are frequent in their visits) are rather bugbears than realities. A few scarlet-coated aides-de-camp, Messieurs Collier and Crawfurd, part of the number, are more likely to break up our retirement, and possibly my Lord himself in his morning's ride; but he shakes his head when I talk of a bed. Alas! it was at Paradise that I may almost say I last saw poor Anguish.[1]

---

[1] Anguish was a young man who had come out with Lord Macartney to the Cape, and had been made Comptroller of the Customs with a salary of 1,000*l.* a year.

He was a good-humoured, easy-tempered young man, whom we were all disposed to love, and who promised fair to contribute to the pleasures of our society. I asked him to go with me to look at this cottage at the time that we saw it was attainable. I never saw him in better spirits. He and I used often to laugh with each other at the 'Malcontents,' as we called them—the English who grumbled about the Cape—he finding novelties and amusements everywhere, as I did, and as Barrow did. 'I think,' said he, 'if the Comptroller of the Customs was to be master of this little place, which some folks would call miserable, he would be contented to give up London and remain here quietly and lazily all his days.' He then went on to say how much more comfortable he now was than he ever had been, that his income was fixed equal to his best hopes through your and Lord Macartney's kindness, and that from its date he even now possessed a little matter to make him clear with the world. In short, I thought him rather a happy man. He was not, however, altogether in good health, as I afterwards heard, and had been taking some medical prescriptions. I thought by a transient glance I had of him one day soon after that his countenance seemed heated and confused, but I never saw him again. He left universal regret behind him, and the full conviction that mental malady had been produced by bodily malady only; for he had done nothing to reproach himself with. I never cease thinking of him when I drive past his grave, which must be passed on going to the Review ground.

Talking of Reviews—the troops here, I fancy, are esteemed to be in fine order. To me they appear well-dressed, well-matched men, and better-looking than any of the lately raised regiments I saw in England. I hear of no disturbances, and sleep secure every night in the garrison with 700 men. Desertion is over, and many of those that had deserted are returned since the proclamation; amongst others, a man who has been absent above a year, and who bears an unlettered testimony to a matter which has been doubted—the existence of the unicorn [1] in the interior parts of Africa. Some years ago, some of the natives had expressed their surprise at seeing it in the King's arms, and when they were asked if they would procure such an animal for a sum of money they had shuddered, saying, 'Ay, to be sure,' but he was 'their god.' This soldier's evidence corroborates this; he describes the unicorn to be much larger than a horse, though less than a small elephant; about as high, he said, as the room. He had on shoes made of the hide of one; they are of immoderate strength, and the skin more of the horse-hide sort than of any other.

Mr. Barrow, who has gone up the country to the bushmen's land, will, may be, see something of this animal; but he will be chiefly in quest of a still better thing—a good silver or gold mine. Of the first

[1] This must be the rhinoceros.

there is no doubt of there being several, and containing a much greater quantity of silver than is to be found in any of the mines we have in England. I hear there are also gold mines ; if we could pay off our *paper debt* with some of this, and hand you over some to pay off your National Debt, it would be pretty.[1] Mr. Barrow is to bring me down a little girl from a particular country, far, far in the inner parts of this wide continent, where the people do not exceed four feet in stature and females have little pads or footboards behind, which serve for a seat for their children, instead of carrying them on their shoulders. They are clever and faithful, I hear.[2]

The day before yesterday a sad accident happened, or rather a wicked act, the son of our butcher being killed by his slave in revenge for having been refused liberty to go out on Sunday, though it was *not* his turn to do so. After he had stabbed him he attempted to murder his mistress, and stabbed one of her slaves. I suppose the unfortunate wretch would have ' run muck ' (as is the term in this country of frenzy from despair and the certainty of death), and would have killed every one he met, (it is some years since an instance of this kind has happened) ; but the man had been wounded in his attempts, and must have died, had not his life been cut short by the gallows an hour after the affair happened, to deter others.

---

[1] The paper currency of the Colony amounted to 258,255*l.*, and there was at first no metallic coin in circulation.
[2] The aborigines of South Africa were pigmies.

Thank God, the days of torture are over, and the sad evidences of what *was* practised by the Dutch Government only remain on a high ground hard by the entrance to the Castle ; it froze my blood at first, but habit hardens the nerves, I hope without hardening the heart.

I have had a visit at the Castle from one of the Kaffir chiefs, with his train of wives and dogs ; he was as fine a morsel of bronze as I ever saw, and there ought to have been a pair of them with candlesticks in their hands. Nothing could exceed the savages' notes, which accompanied their uncouth gestures in their warlike dances. I gave them many trifles, and the chief a cap, which pleased him so much that with the gallantry of nature he came forward, and on receiving it from the balcony in the courtyard kissed my hand respectfully. I had prepared some dinner for them, but found they could eat nothing but beef or mutton ; pies, fowls, and still more particularly *fish*, they seemed to have no taste for—indeed, till they reached the Cape they had never seen a fish, hooks and lines being unknown to them, and the fish therefore in their rivers live unmolested by the wiles of Creation's lords. Wine they liked, but rum transported them. I have tried, but at present vainly, to get ostrich feathers. All have been bought up to send to Europe before they reached the Cape—at least since I arrived. *A propos*—should you have any friends coming here, I give you and them this general advice, to bring everything from

London that is necessary for the consumption of one year—Indian goods as well as other things. Nothing here is likely to be soon as cheap as it may be bought in town; nothing is of the best quality; and most things are, by tacit or perhaps private agreement of the possessors, kept up to an immoderate price. There is a man at Simon's Town, one Trail, in one of the public departments (a great rogue), who buys up everything the moment the ships come in, and then puts his own price on the goods, according to the necessities of others. *N.B.*—By his office he is debarred from what he practises. Mr. Barnard wrote to beg that he would ask a little lump sugar from one of the captains of the ships lately arrived, and that Mr. Green would pay for it. Mr. Trail was 'fortunate enough,' he said, to have obtained some 'already,' at only 4*s.* 6*d.* per pound. Mr. Green wisely declined this precious sugar. Could coals be brought out they would answer well, also some grates and portable kitchens. Whoever means to settle here should bring everything, furniture in particular; but it should come out packed in little compass. I brought all my chairs in pieces tied up closely—iron Windsor, and rush-bottom chairs. Carpets and blankets are also necessary, for winter is winter here, and nothing but avarice prevents all from having fires this 11th day of July. But a fire is a serious matter.

This day signals have appeared of the arrival of six more ships, and three Indiamen are at present at

Simon's Town. I hope this new fleet contains my brother Hugh [1]—it will be a joyful meeting! I have not mentioned the arrival of Mr. and Lady Anne Dashwood. She is a sister of Lord Lauderdale, a sweet, good girl who has performed a very heavy duty in my opinion—though it does not seem to strike her as such—in following, or rather accompanying, here a husband whose dreadful countenance bears awful testimony to a vitiated mind and person. Thank God he has contrived to give her such an account of the *How* he happens to be in this state as renders it less shocking to her; but in my opinion his ugly face is more tolerable than the unprincipled, democratic, and free maxims which fall from his lips, and which prevent pity from alleviating the natural disgust the man inspires. It has been necessary to hint to him that some of his doctrines are better kept to himself here, and I believe he has said less of late.

[1] The Hon. Hugh Lindsay, who was in the sea-service of the East India Company.

IV

The Castle, Cape of Good Hope:
September 12th, 1797.

WE have now quite settled down at our residence in the Castle, my dear Friend, and like it very much. I have arranged it all as best I can, a few things we brought out with us from old England coming in most useful, and really the effect is very pleasing to the eye. Since I got our house in order I have been busy carrying out a desire which I know you have much at heart, that we should conciliate as far as we could the factiousness of the Dutch here, which cannot be accomplished by any other means than by mixing them as much as possible in our society. To fulfil my position here as the woman, in the absence of Lady Macartney, at the head of the Government, it is my duty to show civility and hospitality to all the women, Dutch or English, who live on good terms with their husbands, and to all the Dutchmen who have taken the oath of allegiance to his Majesty, and are of sufficient respectability to visit at the Castle. Mr. Barnard has invited the heads of the Departments to dinner, and the dinner went off in excellent style, our Swiss cook doing very well, assisted by three or four female slaves, whom his Excellency gave us permission to have from the Slave Lodge as servants. The balls and parties were left for me to settle as I thought best. Mr. Barnard, however, wished me to consult the Fiscal as to the proper mode of inviting the Dutch ladies. I did so, but found that, though an honest man, he was prejudiced, and if I followed his advice I should keep the friends the Government had already 'twas true, but I should never make any new ones. When I went down the list with him he threw in so many objections to persons whom he called ' disaffected ' that I feared none would be left, and said so. 'Oh,' he said, 'leave it to me, and you shall have at your parties true friends of the Government.' 'But remember,' said I, 'we are come out here not to call the righteous but sinners to repentance, if I may say so without being profane.' 'Well,' he said, 'if you are determined to bring the sheep and the goats together in one fold you must take the chance of your party becoming a beargarden.' 'But I am going to give a ball,' I said, '*mon ami*; and music hath charms to soothe the savage breast.' He laughed and gave way, and so I had things as I wished.

The result is that I have given a most capital party on the 3rd of this month, and shall have one the first Thursday in every month. It is true, some of the Dutch fathers of families were sulky and stayed at home, being lukewarm, I suspect, to the English Government; but the mothers and daughters came, and to plough with heifers has always been reckoned a good means to improve reluctant soil. By-and-by I shall get the fathers, you will see. I had a fiddle or two and a bit of supper after; all went most friendly. The 'hop' gave me also the opportunity of obliging the juvenile part of the Army and Navy, who, as I have told you, have been kept much in the background by their commanding officers. The invitations were conveyed through the mediums of the colonels of the Army and captains of the Navy to the subaltern officers, and thus all of them who were best behaved and most gentlemanlike were sent, and I think enjoyed themselves thoroughly, flirting a good deal with the Dutch ladies, who did not seem to share their fathers' dislike of English officers. I shall have a similar party on the first Thursday of every month, as I have already told you, but cannot have public days oftener, as everything is so very, very dear that I should be ruined. You will easily believe this, my dear friend, when I tell you that, amongst other things, my thirsty guests drank me up five dozen of porter, a little stock of which I had brought with me, but not enough to stand many such attacks. As to supper, three or four hams, some dozens of fowls and ducks, venison, and other game vanished in the twinkling of an eye, along with pastry of all sorts, for supper is a great meal here. I was able, however, to carry out the lighting on a more economical plan than at home. Our lamps, which were numerous, were lighted, and well lighted, with the tails of the sheep whose saddles we were eating. About these saddles of mutton, it occurred to me before leaving England that it might be useful to carry with me to Africa a map of a sheep and an ox, as I thought it likely that the Dutch butchers might cut their meat up awkwardly. I was not mistaken; my maps have been of great assistance to me here.

About the third part of the ladies at my party were Dutch—not more; but I shall have more by-and-by. Some of our Dutch ladies, in the town especially, are not all that they should be. The French, I am told, corrupted them; the English have merely taught them to affect virtue. I fear, alas! too, that some of our officers have led them astray from it. I cannot shut my eyes to the fact. So far as I hear, this is a great place for marriages, and our brides generally lay in with fine boys about two months after marriage, so rapid are things in this country. When I was told this, wishing to be polite, I said that I feared the children had come a little too soon. 'Not at all, madam,' said the Dutchman, answering literally, 'they came exactly at the proper time, but the marriages took place a little late.' I love a delicate distinction, but on his part the humour was quite unconscious.

I hope at my next party to have a more numerous Dutch collection, as they will then understand that they may come without invitation. You will remember how angry you were with me, my dear friend, and how you sent me that *horrible* letter, when I wrote to you saying that, though Mr. Barnard and myself were most grateful for all your kindness in obtaining this appointment, 'the prettiest appointment,' to quote your own words, ' a young man could wish,' I took exception to the word 'Secretary,' because I feared the situation would imply a certain amount of inferiority among people who did not properly understand. Well, my fears have come true. It will make you smile to tell you that many of the Dutch women declined paying me the first visit, because I was not of high enough rank to receive it. I find they used to visit the Governor's wife and the Councillors' wives, but not the Secretary's wife, first; and though I am the only woman belonging to the Government, yet I am but *Madame la Secrétaire*, you know, to them. As I looked on this rather as an evasion to keep off from visiting in the Castle at all (as they supposed I might stand on the ceremony of putting myself on the footing of the Governor's lady, there being no lady but myself), I took it quite easily on another plan, and said that, though it was the custom in England for native residents always to visit strangers first, yet, if visiting the residents first would be considered by them as any conciliatory mark of respect on my part, I was perfectly ready to do so; and off I set with a volley of visits to some of the first people, declaring myself an enemy to all forms which in a small society kept respectable people at a distance from each other.

Fortunately I visited only two or three, who from sickness were confined at home, or who, from little circumstances that had passed, I ought to have called on to thank them for having put their daughters under my protection at my party and *Hop*; for in answer to a few lines I wrote to the Fiscal on this subject, begging to know his opinion, I find by his reply—sensibly and prettily expressed—that I shall do best to let it alone, and a little time and my now well-known disposition to be well with them will effect the matter as far as it need be effected.

General Dundas and some officers with him have been up the country for ten days. I have just seen one of them. He tells me that at a distance from Cape Town there is by no means the scarcity there is at the Cape, and they bought grain for three dollars a sack which here costs eleven dollars. This leads one to hope that time, and the confidence of the Boers in finding a market, may render everything cheaper this ensuing year. I'll let this remain open till the last day, *cher ami*. I mean to go to Simon's Bay with my brother Hugh, to see him on board, and I shall then be able to say something of it.

Wednesday, September 16th.—Since I concluded the last page we have had a gallant whaler here, who with twenty-four men (as I hear) has taken a Dutch ship from Batavia, laden with arms and ammunition.[1]

---

[1] A capture made by the 'Hope' South Sea whaler in Delagoa Bay of a Dutch brig that was coming with a supply of arms and ammunition for the Dutch malcontents at Graaf Reinet.

It required *finesse* as well as courage to effect this matter, but I heartily rejoice that we have got part of the powder and have destroyed the rest of it, as the people at Graaf Reinet (for which it was bound) are very ill affected. Mr. Barrow, I believe, is there by this time; I fancy he will be able to give many judicious accounts in various ways. We have had a south-easter these two days, and a pretty strong one, which has delayed the loading of the ships with victuals for the convoy in False Bay. I hope all will reach you safe when they do sail, for great must be the riches of this Fleet. I have got a jar of pineapples from Batavia for Lady Jane, and one for Lady Hardwicke,[1] but I fear much that I shall find it difficult to get them conveyed, the captains are so fearful of taking what they tell me will more than probably bring them to disgrace by being spoiled or lost at the India House. I'll make another trial; it vexes me to see my charming pines here, when I wish them on your table, though you have probably more of these things than you care about—no, I retract; if it is difficult now to get such things safely landed, it must have been more difficult before I wish I knew the best mode of sending them—whether by an Indian ship, letting them take their chance, or by a man-o'-war. I'll try Mr. Brice, Mrs. Anstruther's brother, a modest, pleasing young man who has lately been with us; *smuggled*, I find they must be.

[1] Lady Anne's sister.

September 24*th*.—We have been at False Bay since I concluded the above, seeing Hugh on board. I find the place rather better-looking than I expected, the houses on the outside being, as is the Dutch fashion, all well whitewashed, with their clean shirts on. But there is sadly little room for the poor sick fellows, the honest Tars, multitudes of whom have been lost for want of air and wholesome accommodation, they having been so closely packed in their hospital with scurvy, ulcers, etc., that it was certain death going into it. Of late, the physician to the Navy (Dr. Pattison) has got, with *much* difficulty, leave to have the use of a stable for horses belonging to some of the officers residing there; and since then sixty men have been put into it, and many of them have recovered. What a pity that more places are not erected for them! With the expenditure of a very little money hundreds, ay, thousands, of people would be saved in this hot climate. What fools, or what dirty, nasty calculators some of the contractors for the public must be! Where is the hospital for the Navy *here* in Cape Town placed? Above the public ovens, where all the bread used in the place is baked, and where the languishing creatures are baked into the next world along with it. But 'tis better to growl *here* than to you across the Bay of Biscay. I have been trying to persuade some of the wise people to give a great lump of the mountain behind the house at False Bay to some old honourable seaman to become gardener and raise vegetables for the use of the Navy, selling them at a small price, yet getting a good livelihood too. Every potato and cabbage at an immoderate price comes from Cape Town twenty miles over the bad roads, and at a rate that Government can hardly afford to purchase for the sick. How much cheaper, then, the other way would be, and what a benefit![1] There is a Company's garden—Mr. Trail asked it for the above purpose; but since he has had it, the Navy people are the only ones to whom he will not sell a potato, for fear of its being remembered how he got it. (I am told he is now worth 60,000*l*.) He was a favourite of our friend Lord Keith, who certainly must have thought well of him *then*; but he is sadly detested here now for his extraordinary practices. If he is turned out, which there is some talk of (I speak merely of common report), I wish the garden could be turned to the purpose I mention; I'll venture for once to launch a woman's opinion about it.

Certainly it would be very difficult for an enemy to land at Simon's Bay and get on to Cape Town, as the road may be so easily defended by a handful of men—the sea coming close up on the right, the road being bad and narrow and rocky and almost perpendicular, mountains being to the left, on which there are many little batteries raised and cannon

[1] The wisdom of this is evident from the fact that at the mutiny of the squadron at the Cape, which took place shortly after, one of the chief grievances of the sailors was that they were given no vegetable food.

pointed. There is a dangerous pass, too, to cross in one of the small bays, and a quicksand in another. The camp at Meusenberg is formed of huts at present, but the officers are building a better; the situation must be healthy for the men, and easily defended from the reasons I mention. The officers were all out a-shooting, but a soldier gave us a bit of boiled beef, and made us an apology that they had no beer or wine to give us—nothing but Constantia [1]; but when I tasted it, to be sure 'twas excellent. The person who boiled the beef had been steward to the Duke of Orleans; I remarked the man in Paris. Such are the chances of this mortal life! I dare say you think I have digested a democratic morsel, when it was dressed by him. He kept afterwards a club in Dover Street, and is a bad subject in all senses of the word. You would have paused and fixed your eye with a smile on our carriage, had you seen us driving away in our Dutch vehicle, with one black coachman and eight horses; but postillions are unnecessary here, the horses being blessed with a portion of good sense to pick their own steps. It would have surprised you had you seen us at the narrowest passes, bowling away, and passing other carriages and waggon-carts, with eight horses and one driver, yet no harm ensuing. Adieu, Adieu. I know you must think I shall never finish.

I shall not tell you of the alarm of an engagement which frightened many people, but proved at

[1] A Cape wine.

last to be a species of varying clouds over the horizon, which perfectly resembled smoke and vessels at a distance. We think that Admiral Pringle does not dislike the Cape so much since he fell in love with a pretty little Miss; it threatened matrimony for some time, but, like the engagement, it has gone off in misty clouds of smoke and left the weaker vessel unmanned! Again, Adieu.

V

The Castle, Cape Town:
October 15th, 1797.

I HEAR there is a ship sails for England to-day, and I seize the opportunity to tell you, *cher ami*, that we are all well. We are anxious for news from England, as you will easily believe when you know that we first received the accounts of the Mutiny in the Navy by a foreign ship (as I think, Danish), which was corroborated first by one East Indiaman that put in on account of the health of the captain, and afterwards by the fleet bound for Bengal, who were 'short of water.' Perhaps some idea of disposing of investments here beneficially might co-operate. Be that as it may, it was plain to all here that it was not intended that this squadron should touch at the Cape, as it brought letters to no one, except one, dated the 15th of May, to me from Lord St. Helens' sister, recommending a relation to my attention in case of his touching at the Cape; but the date showed that it was written previous to those transactions which afterwards took place. I thank God they have terminated at last in quietness, though I am sorry our Navy has ever showed a spirit so turbulent and rebellious as has been evinced. French politics, of course, have taken the advantage of a disposition to call aloud for redress on matters where perhaps the sailors were justified for grumbling, but which we suppose the French hoped to improve beyond the point they have effected.

Newspapers have reached us in plenty, though nothing else. A peace, talked of as daily likely to take place, meets here with universal belief. The Cape to be ceded,[1] as one article, is almost universally believed by the Dutch; and terms little to the honour of England have been named as necessary to be complied with by us in order to effect a peace, which is supposed to be called aloud for by the country. A change of the Ministry[2] is stated, I see by the papers, and rather credited here, upon the supposition that the present Ministers will not agree to be the makers of what they do not approve of, and also that the French wish rather to negotiate with the *other party*. Should the circumstances of the country be so low, the voice of the people so loud, and the disapprobation of the present Ministry so great to the terms proposed that they will not complete the peace—which, however, upon the whole is settled to take place—I suppose you will all walk out at one door of the stage while another set of better disposed men walk in at the other, who, after

---

[1] It was ceded to the Dutch five years later by the Peace of Amiens.
[2] Pitt's First Administration.

finishing *their* job, will follow you out at the first
door and you will come back at the second. This,
unless some new man willing to do the business is
incorporated with a part of the old body for that
purpose, I suppose will be the case, because I hear
others suppose it. As to my poor little impressions
and expectations, I can neither believe in a peace (at
least not in the course of this year) nor in any
change of Ministry ; and if there is a peace I don't
much believe that the Cape will be made any great
point of by the French. It will cost them money to
keep it, and, unless they wish to send a great many
of their unnecessary troops out of the country to
prevent disturbances at home, I don't much see why
they should wish for it, except with a future view of
taking India from us. But they have plenty of
work to do nearer home before they come to that.

There is plainly a fashion in everything in this
world. The English Mutiny,[1] of course, has set the
fashion here, and we have had a swinging mutiny
of our own at Simon's (False) Bay. Delegates from
the malcontents at home came out, it appears, in the
'Arniston,' and, working on the minds of the seamen,
who only knew the progress but not the event of the
Mutiny at the Nore, a mutiny here broke out on board
the Admiral's ship this day fortnight. The Admiral
dined with us the day before, and we saw something
after dinner made him uneasy, but Lord Augustus

[1] The Mutiny which broke out in the fleet on May 7th of this year
(1797), commonly called the Mutiny at the Nore.

Fitzroy,[1] who came from the Bay, knew of nothing amiss; he was also of the party. They both left Cape Town next day, Captain Stephens having come thence on the business, who by the bye had been turned out of the 'Tremendous' by the crew, who have a particular dislike to both captains of that name, we know not with what justice. Admiral Pringle and Lord Augustus each went on board his particular ship, but found that the orders of the delegates *only* were to be attended to till such time as certain grievances were redressed. Meantime all the commanders but the Stephens's were treated with the usual respect except in allowing them no command. This disgusted most of them, and from (probably natural) feelings of injured pride they quitted their ships and declared them severally in a state of rebellion. Not so Tod —lately appointed to the 'Trusty'—a man who has risen from a very low class of life by undisputed merit in his profession; he saw the thing (as I can't help thinking) in a better point of view, and remained on board his ship, watching the moment when the lassitude which follows an intemperate exertion should render it possible to make a few of his men listen to reason. Meantime, the other captains were all on shore until a signal from the Admiral's ship to attend him there carried them on board. When there the crew kept all of them prisoners! They fed them well, to be sure, and denied them no mark of attention. But the terms which they offered for reconciliation were, that the two Stephens's

[1] Lord Augustus Fitzroy commanded the *Impérieuse*.

should be sent home to England to be tried for misconduct; that their grievances, which chiefly consisted in their allowances being unfairly withheld by the pursers from them, should be redressed; and that a general pardon to delegates and seamen alike should be granted. On these terms and none other they offered to lay down their arms. And these terms the Admiral would not listen to. The delegates must, he said, be given up, and the Stephens's reinstated.

Meantime all was hurry here, but without much alarm for the event; for at a critical moment a Danish ship arrived, and brought the very happy accounts of all being at last arranged in England, and the punishment of the delegates and others of the party. Nothing could be more fortunate than this news. Some people feared that it might have a contrary effect, and render the crews desperate, already possessed of power to do almost what they chose, but the event proved it to be different. The seamen really had some grievances to complain of, and, with hope to find them righted, they were willing to shake hands and be friends with their commanders, though the delegates had certainly intended the matter to go much farther.

I must here introduce, in jest, a little anecdote of General Dundas. He left Cape Town for Simon's Bay as quickly as the occasion demanded him, but no one could get him convinced that the crews could be so headstrong and intemperate as he was told they were, particularly on the 'Tremendous,' which he was determined to go on board of. 'They only want talking round calmly,' said he, 'not minding their nonsense, but arguing the matter coolly and reasonably with them.' Some of his military friends smiled at the idea of his supposing himself more particularly qualified than certain others to talk a mutiny over coolly, and they fortunately persuaded him against going on board, else both Admiral and Commander-in-Chief would have been prisoners.

Meantime all proper steps were taken by the Ordinance Engineers, etc., to entrench the troops, who marched on to Simon's Bay. It would have had but little effect, I suppose, considering what a mouthful the works there would have been to the guns of the 'Tremendous.' At last the ferment flattened, and the Admiral found it best, in order to finish the dangerous business, to compromise the matter—the Stephens's to have a court martial on them here, the pursers to be tried, and all grievances to be redressed. A general pardon to be granted. This last we all were sorry for; even the best-natured people wished the delegates to be made examples of to the Navy. But Admiral Pringle is pretty firm, and I suppose he found that he could not work the point farther than he did.

Women may say anything without presumption. How well I remember saying to the Admiral that if I were he, I should be greatly tempted to tell the Navy that, though I had received no official intelligence from England, yet I was apt to believe that there were certain benefits to be bestowed on the seamen at home, and whatever they were I believed I might confidently assure them that they would share in all such.[1] A few exhilarating words such as these I foolishly thought might have been said by the Admiral without taking too much responsibility on himself or incurring disapprobation at home; but he seemed to think nothing should be taken for granted in public departments, and that he had no right officially to know or say anything. Of course he must be right, as he is a clever man and knows his business; but how often have I not seen (to use a vulgar proverb) 'a stitch in time save nine'! I believe there was a judicious speech issued in the public orders to the Army within these few days, which will have a good effect. They all expect, I presume, what is not, however, promised in it. Something is needed here for the poor military, for things still remain sadly dear, and I fear the Dutch heads will contrive to keep them so by their manœuvres, though there is the prospect of a harvest plentiful beyond what has been known, owing to the immense quantity of rain which has lately fallen and swelled out the heads of the corn in a manner that Madam Nature is not accustomed to experience at the Cape, for this is a dry season in general.

---

[1] Lady Anne was right. The mutiny at home was eventually quelled by judicious concessions and the personal influence of Lord Howe with the seamen.

What will you say when I tell you that I am writing to you in bed? I had very near met with the ugly accident of being killed a few days ago. The servant had somehow been out of the way, and the coachman got off the box to open the carriage. I am always a coward of horses standing at their own discretion without a governor—Cape horses especially are not to be trusted. I called to him to go to their heads; but they did not wait, and off they set round the circle, or parade, in the garrison. As I could not guess where they might land me, or whether they might not overturn me at a sharp angle in running to their stables, and as the door was open and the step down, I was tempted to jump out, and, thank God, I felt ground. But I felt no more for some time. The carriage came round safe to the door, galloping, but no Lady Anne; I was found in the middle of the circle laying on my back, my head cut, and insensible. I recovered myself, however, in a quarter of an hour; my shoulder and ankle were both bruised, and my head had a considerable contusion on it; but the doctor, who by the bye is a right good man (Pattison), said there was no fracture; so for anything else there's no great matter. I have lain in bed these two days, and am now going to rise, bones whole. Take this, however, as an apology for all the errors this letter may contain; for what can be expected from a woman with a plaister on her pericranium?

What a bold south-easter we have had these two

days! How the wind raged, and how a tall tree which is in the courtyard before my windows bent and tossed its great branches in at the casement, where the wind blew out a pane every half-hour! I shall feel more of these winds, I hear. How I long, my dear friend, for letters now, to tell me how you all are!—if safe and prosperous, or invaded by a foreign foe. I long also to know what is to become of us little mortals at the extreme point of Africa.

The last month has sent in from the country quantities of waggons chiefly loaded with wine, butter, skins, feathers, and oranges—grain is sometimes added as the farmer happens to have it. The waggons are very narrow, about the size of a large pipe of wine, and long enough to hold three in length. They are drawn by sixteen oxen, and driven by one man, a Hottentot besides generally walking at the head of the first pair. To govern their bullocks they have whips of immense length, which they lay on and produce no small effect; one lash is quite enough to set all the team into motion. These animals are much larger than our general breed of bullocks in England. I made a tallish man try the height of one of them—he guessed the team at sixteen hands and a-half. The men who drive them are in proportion to their cattle, of a very large and robust stature, but their countenances gentle, and nothing rude or boisterous in their manners.

I long most ardently now to get up the country a

little. I shall try hard for it when I am quite well, which I expect will be in a day or two. I have two offers—the offer of good living, lodging, carriages, and civil hospitality from the Landdrost of Stellenbosch,[1] and the offer of an empty house, two beds, and five chairs from the Fiscal, who has a house in that village, inhabited only by mice, and of course by no means uninhabited by *fleas*—the empty houses here being always richly stocked with that sort of wild animal. I love liberty, and believe I shall prefer the mice and the fleas, a ' conjurer' for my cook, and the power of doing what I like, to the good things the Landdrost proffers me, with the hospitable attentions of his wife and daughters, which I shall gladly accept of now and then, but not all day long.

The brig which was sent round to Graaf Reinet to meet Barrow is returned. The first lieutenant sleeps here, and tells all he saw to my lord and master, but I haven't been stout enough to see him myself yet. He describes that part of the country as extremely cheap and extremely plentiful. Some of the Dutch Boers, he mentions, drink wine. Pitchers of milk are put on table after dinner by way of beverage; there ought to be beautiful shepherdesses and true shepherds at that board, as it surely portrays the Golden Age!

All your friends here are well; one of the last times I was in company with Lord Macartney he

---

[1] The stipendiary magistrate of the district, who received the revenue and administered justice.

danced a reel remarkably well to the Scots' bagpipes with Lady Anne Dashwood, Mrs. Campbell, and a brigade-major. Perhaps you think this is cross reading, or a puzzle, or conundrum; but no such thing—it is true. He was in excellent spirits, and paid a compliment to 'the Laddies' ain piper' and the reel of Tulloch which neither the general nor the transported piper will soon forget. I dare not add, what I believe is true too, that I fear the little twinge in the toe next day whispered to his Excellency that he had been rash.

October 30*th*.—I missed the ship, and have kept this open therefore to give you the latest news about the mutiny here. As I said before, it was generally regretted that the Admiral was obliged to give a general pardon, especially to the delegates, as the consequence of their escaping punishment has been seen since, in that the Blue Jacket (the sign of mutiny) has been hung up in two of the vessels from St. Helena, the 'Raisonable' and the 'Sphinx.' It is now taken down, though a strong disposition appeared in the fleet to set off anew. Subordination is by no means established; the ferment is working secretly still, and with a degree of intrigue and plan in it that seems to originate from cleverer heads than those of the mere John Bulls, who are only the tools. The sailors come on shore in numbers, parties of twelve at a time; they pillage the markets, get drunk, riot, and endeavour by every means to corrupt the Army; their bad influence began to be felt, and

General Dundas wisely ordered the Army to be encamped. This was done at twenty-four hours' warning, and near Rondebosch, which is six miles distant from Green Point, where the sailors often land, and four from the Cape. The General and Lord Macartney saw it indispensably necessary to break the dangerous friendship forming between the Army and Navy by this move. Now the troops have something to do, and that is in favour of the continuation of their loyal principles. All the garrison has marched out but a company or two; so we are solitary enough, but have no fears, and the sentinels have orders to permit no sailor to pass into the Castle. There was a great wine-house there, where the sailors constantly resorted. The man and woman who kept it we sent off; and six other wine-houses—or punch-houses, as they call them—were broken up by Government the evening before last. Men tell women little truth when there is real or supposed danger in question, therefore I can't well quote anything that I hear from masculine reports; but I fancy that the ferment here will cease in a few days more, without further harm. It has produced only the bad effect of forcing a measure (the encampment of the Army) which I suppose must cost money.

I now go on with my monthly ball, and have had all the respectable Dutch families round in turn to dinner. I believe I may tell you very honestly that in our different departments Mr. Barnard and I are very great favourites of the Dutch inhabitants. We are both very civil, and never despise anybody, which I can perceive has been one great error in some of the English. I was asked to a ball given at a Dutch house on account of a wedding the day before yesterday. The parties were a lady of a certain age, with 8,000*l.* or 10,000*l.*—which is here a rarity, the women having little money—the man Mr. Bianchi, an Italian who came out with Sir George Elphinstone.[1] They were half-married the day of the ball—that is to say (for I know you are beginning to laugh), they went to be examined by the notary; two or three weeks hence the ceremony takes place. It was an excellent ball, and voluminous supper. To be sure, the Dutch women don't flirt with the English officers!! I say nothing. Mr. Bianchi says that his future is very ugly and old, but she is rich, sensible, and good-humoured, and he'll contrive to be happy enough. I mention this in case Lord K. should like to know particulars. She is not a favourable likeness of Lady Grantham, but has a resemblance. Adieu, *mon cher ami,* I must conclude. All your friends here are well. Sir James Craig is arrived safely at Bombay. It is thought he is not a likely man to live long in Indian climates—he is very fat, and lives very high. Perhaps you know that there are seven provinces in China in a state of mutiny. The China ships bring this news. Barrow

---

[1] Admiral Elphinstone was in command of the sea-forces which helped to capture the Cape in 1795.

writes in raptures of Kaffir Land and of the king—a young man of twenty, who is pleased with his visit and glad to treat on terms of friendship with us. God bless you.

VI

The Castle, Cape of Good Hope:
November 29th, 1797.

THE last ships, my dear Friend, have sailed without any letter from me to you. I had made myself sure of finding them still here on my return from the country, where we have lately had the pleasure of spending a very interesting fortnight. It is the first time since we arrived, now seven months ago, that Mr. Barnard has taken the indulgence of a little country air. I should hardly mention this as an indulgence granted to himself, he having been sent to Stellenbosch by Lord Macartney to enforce the Oath of Allegiance, which has been constantly evaded by certain *mauvais sujets* who live there, in number about a dozen.

Friday the 10th of this month being the last day granted by the second Proclamation, it was necessary for Mr. Barnard to leave Cape Town on the 9th, the very morning when the Admiral gave his ultimatum to those in mutiny on board his and the other ships. Two hours was the time he allowed for them to give up their delegates and return to their duty, or by pulling down his flag to declare open rebellion, in which case the batteries were instantly to have fired on

them. This circumstance had been concealed fro[m]
the ladies till we were a couple of miles out of tow[n]
when Mr. Barnard told us of it, and also that t[he]
two hours were within ten minutes of being expire[d]
I need not say how anxiously some of us stretch[ed]
our throats out of the Dutch cabriole we were in [to]
look back on the Bay, where still—still as we looked—
the Admiral's flag floated, and a few minut[es]
before the time was finally over we heard a gu[n]
which led us to send back one of our servants [to]
bring us the news, well authenticated, in the eve[n]ing. We hoped the best; nor were we disappoint[ed]
in the end, each ship coming to the resolution [of]
sacrificing its ringleader rather than being blow[n]
into the air by the artillery placed against [it].
Twenty-one mistaken fellows, blind agents of Fren[ch]
miscreants, were brought on shore, all of the[m]
daring and fearless of the event, which is not [as]
yet brought to its final issue.

As the little tour which this absence from t[he]
Cape permitted us to make is the first good oppo[r]tunity I have as yet had of seeing the country a[nd]
being able in any degree to form a judgment of t[he]
Boers, or real Dutch settlers—the people at Ca[pe]
Town being scarcely to be named as such—I will gi[ve]
my dear friend a short account of things as the[y]
presented themselves to me, always trusting th[at]
you will forgive ten thousand inaccuracies a[nd]
frivolities, while I repeat matters that, even at [a]
distance, you have a more just idea of, I dare sa[y]

from your better information, than any I can give you.

Our road from Cape Town to Stellenbosch was not distinguished by much variety. We went by the Koyle, a long sandy hill, having first passed the Salt *rivière*, and that long tract of sandy common (if I may call it so) that bears many traces of having one or two hundred years ago been covered by the sea, but which is now only covered scantily by heaths, and such plants and brushwood as partake a little of both sea and land. But as every plant, bush, and tree in this country has its flower and fruit at some season of the year, even in the barrenest soils there are novelty and entertainment to the eye which has never seen the thing before. We passed a considerable number of waggons loaded with wine, as is the case at this time of the year; each of them had sixteen oxen to draw it, but were just then without any, as the cattle had been turned out to graze amidst the bushes, where it was lucky if they could pick up anything, as these poor animals never taste food or drink from the time they enter Cape Town till they leave it, which is often two days, if the wine they have brought happens not to be immediately disposed of. Certainly there must be something rich in the dry herbs of the soil here, for the oxen are now as fat as they can be, and yet I have nowhere seen the appearance of verdure, except the verdure of green barley or other corn, for there is no grass anywhere. What they have to draw seems quite ludicrous behind sixteen great beasts—simply one or two barrels of wine, which I fancy does not amount to above three pipes, and which we should reckon four oxen quite equal to. I have often wondered why they don't sell a dozen of the sixteen when they come to the Cape, and return with four; but their honour and respectability amongst the Boers (and this exists in a still greater degree amongst the Kaffirs) is to have an immense number of cattle. The drivers are a race of men as large in proportion as their oxen, which is much above the size of the European breed. One man drives the whole, another taking care of the casks and being ready to assist in case of accident. I believe I have mentioned part of this before—no matter.

As we drove along, we saw our only English dog who has survived the ailment which attacks all who arrive here, and who is a stout vulgar pointer called 'Chops,' pointing at something, running back to the carriage, returning, and pointing again. Mr. Barnard said that the dog had not his usual manner, but a mixture of fear with his alacrity, so he went with his gun, and found Chops pointing at a serpent of between five and six feet long. Mr. Barnard killed it with his whip, and I have kept its skin.

The Landdrost of Stellenbosch,[1] as I told you, had pressed us to come to his house. He has two pretty daughters and a good-humoured wife, but

[1] Ryno Johannes van der Riet, who had been appointed by General Craig.

the ladies could neither *spraken* English nor French, and as we have never before found any necessity of speaking Dutch, we consequently are ignorant of it. I therefore preferred accepting of the Fiscal's empty house in the same village, where I thought we should be more at liberty, and give less trouble; consenting, however, to dine with the Landdrost and his family every day, and to accept of their carriage and horses, together with the most illustrious coachman of old Governor Sheiskin, now theirs, to drive us to all curious sights near or at a distance. We arrived in time to dinner, and had a plentiful one, really good, though in the Dutch style. The Landdrost's house we found more airy and spacious than any other I have been in here, having a sort of second row of rooms behind the first; but the division of every Dutch house in the Colony is the same—namely, a hall, a square room on either hand, and another family eating-room behind, with two bedchambers. Before the Landdrost's door there are the only two fine oaks I have seen, except the others in the village. They each measure eighteen feet round. But the perfection of this place consists in its extreme coolness in the midst of the most sultry weather; it is built in long streets, perfectly regular, each street having on each side a row of large oaks, which shadow the tops of the houses, keeping them cool, and forming a shady avenue between, through which the sun cannot pierce. Whatever way one walks one finds an avenue, right or left, and each house has a good garden. Stellenbosch, therefore, though there may not be above a hundred families in it, covers a good deal of ground, and is so perfectly clean and well-built that it appears to be inhabited only by people of small fortune. But I am told there are many very poor people in it, without the means of ever becoming richer, as during the Dutch Government no manufacture was permitted there, and any person endeavouring to gain a livelihood by such means would have been severely punished. From this cause the place has few young people. It seems rather an asylum for old age than anything else, and I am told people live longer in it than in any other part of the Colony.

At the Fiscal's we found a small clean house on the same little plan with the rest, kept by a black woman, wife to the Landdrost's coachman, she keeping in her turn a slave, who was mother of eight little naked mice that run about the gardens and offices just as they came into the world, without being ashamed. We had a very good bed, partaking, however, of the error of the country, that to be cool a bed should be made of the finest feathers, instead of which a mattress of hair, pretty hard, and covered with leather, is the real luxury.

Next morning, being Friday, I thought I would take a peep at the Landdrost and the ill-affected faces that were to come to take the Oath. As I walked through one of the avenues I was pleased with the singular appearance of innumerable quantities of birds' nests hanging suspended from every bough, built with a hole at the bottom for the birds to enter by. Instinct instructs them to form them so to avoid weasels, monkeys, and serpents, who would otherwise devour the young. The husband bird builds the nest, and it often happens, if he is awkward, that the wife is so much displeased with it that she tears it in pieces, and he has to begin again. Out of twelve Boers who meant to evade swearing allegiance, I found that eight had now taken the Oath and were gone; the others had made various excuses, and had not appeared at all. This being the case, it only remained for Mr. Barnard to give orders for them to be laid hold of. But he thought the more moderate way better, of giving them still two days more, and of going back to the Cape to receive Lord Macartney's further orders. He concluded, however, that he should find it necessary to appoint a party of soldiers to be in the neighbourhood on Saturday evening, and to have very express orders sent to the parties to enforce their attendance on Sunday morning.

I amused myself this day by taking a view of the country and the village from one of the hills. The valley, though not extensive, is rich and fertile were it well cultivated, but the farmers are bad ones. I cannot help thinking that wherever a soil is stony, as it often, is here, dibbling, as they do in Norfolk, would be a good plan. Wine is the chief produce of the land hereabouts, and a small piece of ground only being necessary to make a great deal of wine, the rest of Mother Earth lies barren and neglected. One thousand vines make a barrel of wine, and it contains eight times eighty gallons. The vines are planted in rows, and there seem to be about four feet between vine and vine. To what an extent the cultivation of the vine might be brought here, if the farmers were sure of a good market! At present there is one thing greatly against the improvement of the vine by any better modes than what are used—namely, that wine from the country is bought by the merchant in town at the market price, without any reference to superiority or inferiority of quality. They don't give themselves the trouble to taste it, and sell it off in the same careless way as they buy it.

I never saw the force of prejudice more apparent than in the way Englishmen here turn up their foolish noses at the Cape wines *because* they are Cape wines. They will drink nothing but port, claret, or madeira, pretending that the wines of the country give them bowel-ache! It may be so, if they drink two or three bottles at a time, and that very frequently, but Cape wine will not do so if used in moderation. Mr. Barnard drinks nothing else himself, though we have every other good wine at table, champagne and burgundy excepted. I must tell you, as an illustration, of what happened one day with us after dinner. We had a little hock on board ship, two bottles of which remained over, and we keep them for Lord Macartney when he is ill and wishes for a *bonne bouche*, as they happen to be very fine. After dinner I thought myself drinking up one of the bottles of this hock, and said to Mr. Barnard, 'O fie! why do you give us this to-day- it is some of our fine hock.' A certain lieutenant-colonel, who shall be nameless, on this filled his glass. 'Lord bless me, what fine wine this is!' said he; 'I have not tasted a glass such as this since I came here.' I then found, on asking, that it was Steine wine, a cheap Cape wine, which Mr. Barnard had not liked, and had ordered for common use in the household. In a moment the colonel found fifty faults in it.

On Saturday evening Mr. Barnard returned from Cape Town to Stellenbosch with powers from Lord Macartney to do as he saw best on the spot. Next morning our Jacobins arrived, stout, sulky, democratic fellows, who with wives and children preferred refusing the Oath of Allegiance and going to Batavia to swearing to be honest and quiet members of the community, taking up no arms against us. There was now nothing further to be done—the Landdrost and Mr. Barnard had argued with them till both were worn out with vexation and fatigue. The dragoons then appeared, and the five men, escorted by them, were carried prisoners to the Cape, fully expecting, as a Dutch servant of ours told me who stood by them, to be set at liberty on arriving there, and the matter to blow over. The villagers in general disapproved of their conduct, and the Lady Landdrost, with tears in her eyes, said: 'How can you justify yourselves to your wives and children for this?' But their reason was plain. Fully persuaded that the government of the Cape will not remain long in the hands of the English, they are taking grounds to be great men when the French get possession of it. But they may reckon without their host if they think the French are bound by any tie except what they suppose to be for their own interest.

Being Sunday, we went to church here, though we understood not a word of the language. What amazing people for fat some of these good people are! A tendency to dropsy at the same time perhaps increases it, but after thirty years of age it is rare to see a woman, in the lower class of life particularly, weighing less than from twelve to fifteen stone. The clergyman's wife, talking of the number of children christened in the parish, told me that the Sunday before this there had been twelve children baptized, and only five mothers to those twelve! Two of the mothers had three each, and three others two each. 'I thought, madam,' said I, 'that twins even had been rare in this country.' 'Oh no, madam,' she replied, 'I had two myself but four months ago.' These prolific mothers came from Overbergh; behind those mountains all sorts of good things are, I hear, to be found. I wonder the

Dutch allowed such a race to live, their Government being equally against population and cultivation. I believe it is a bit of a reflection on people here to have no family. One or two Dutchmen, on hearing us say we had none, exclaimed, 'Oh, miserable! miserable!' in such a doleful tone, that I think I shall give myself credit for half a dozen left at school for the future.

On Monday Mr. Barnard returned to the Cape for a day, and Anne Barnard and I took the opportunity of going into Hottentot Holland to see a famous pass in the mountains called Hottentot Kloof, which one of our English magazines pencil as tremendous. The day was cold (indeed, as yet we have had no heat to complain of), but it was better so than if it had scorched us. Still the same want of cultivation appeared, with a soil which, as far as my poor share of farming knowledge goes, would be equal to any fair crop that could be required from it. But why raise grain unless there is a market for it? I was sorry to find the season of flowers over—the spring here is a short one, and the flowers are soon dried up and withered by the summer sun. I dug up a few bulbs, which I send to Lady Jane. I know not if they are curious, but the colour was bright and handsome, and I have accompanied them with a few seeds which I cannot vouch for, except that the seed is good, for though the flowers do not change their shapes, they change their colours, and what was scarlet last year may be yellow, blue, or white this. The green flower struck me as being singularly genteel. I shall endeavour to get the finest plants of the sort for her, but meantime she shall have part of what I have procured, with my love, and must be godmother to the flower, which I have called the 'Lady Jane.'

But to return to my little tour. Hottentot Holland we found totally uninhabited by Hottentots, they, poor things, having been driven up the country by their avaricious masters; and nothing can better prove the grasping hope of each Dutchman to possess himself of large domains than the distance at which the settlers have placed themselves from each other, instead of placing their houses within the vicinity of rational society. The Boer or farmer has only thought of keeping himself as little circumscribed as possible, and as far away as he could from the Landdrost's eye. The consequence of this has been that whenever families have settled wide of each other, there has been but a poor increase of them, whereas in places where they have been more confined there is ten times the increase, as in Graaf Reinet. Twenty years ago there were a hundred families in that district; they were not permitted to emigrate beyond a certain distance, and are now eight hundred. In Hottentot Holland there seemed to be a house and farm every mile, or mile and a-half, but no hamlet or village. As the land is cultivated by slaves, and as they are the property of the master, his house has generally a slave-house belonging to it, which, alas! is in place of that happier cottage at home where each Englishman has his wife, his child, his pig, and his cat or dog, as great within its four walls as any emperor within his palace. Until we see here hamlets also raising up their humble heads, and the artificer receiving his shilling or two a day for his work, and spending it as he pleases, unlashed by any rattan, or without any chastisement but his wife's tongue if he has spent too much in porter, we will not see this a flourishing country. At present unwilling drudgery toils, unthanked, for indolent apathy!

The second largest house in Hottentot Holland was purchased lately by a Mr. Thibaud, a Frenchman, and I believe he is supposed to have a hankering after the doctrines of that nation; it is situated near a lake, and that lake is within a mile of Modergal Bay. I mention it particularly as the lake is famous for a fish called the springer, the very best fish I ever tasted in all my life, the most delicate and the fattest. We are in negotiation to procure its breed, and its spawn. I should be delighted were the great events of his Majesty's reign to have added to the list of occurrences the acquisition of 'that charming fish the springer, introduced into this country by the wife of Secretary Barnard.' It weighs about three or four pounds, but fancy cannot paint how good it is—it is the fish only that could convince you. I found the horrors of the kloof, like most other things repeated by those who love to astonish others, very much exaggerated. It is, to be sure, a very narrow steep road cut from the side of a mountain, but I do not think it more terrible than Penmaenmawr in Wales; this last is rather the more frightful of the two in my opinion, as the sea rolls below the rock, but the other may be the more dangerous on account of the badness of the road in ascending, and there is no wall or guard to prevent one from tumbling down the precipice should an accident happen. As I saw this object of fear grow less and less the nearer I approached to it, I stopped to take my sketch of it at some little distance; in this I hear I was wrong, as it appears the most terrible when on it. On t'other side of the mountain there grew a profusion of what are called everlasting flowers, some of which I shall send to Lady Jane. The white remain for ever the same; the red ones are the most curious, being as bright as if made of red foils, but the foolish flowers after being plucked, instead of remaining as they were, or withering, spread from bud to flower, shed bad seed, and fall to pieces. I must kill them by some preparation after they are plucked.

Next day Mr. Barnard returned to Stellenbosch again from the Cape. Our Dutch friends are safe lodged in the Castle till a ship is ready to take them to Batavia—silly, bold, foolish people.[1] No African

---

[1] At the eleventh hour they thought better of it, and took the Oath of Allegiance to King George III. They were set at liberty, but were placed under military supervision for a time,

was ever known to live there. Europeans sometimes do, though rarely. What a pity that so fine a town and country should have so shocking a climate! We now arranged another party which promised to be still pleasanter—namely, to Paarl, a village at the bottom of mountains so called from two enormous stones being at the top of them of a size so immense that it took a friend of mine half an hour to walk round one of them. They are, however, each entire stones, somewhat shaped like imperfect pearls, and awful from gigantic and unique singularity; they are of granite, and one of them is hollow. It is supposed it could contain 20,000 men, but this must be nonsense—let us call it 1,000, and then I shall have a better chance of being believed. The valley beneath is rich, fertile, and pretty, being tolerably wooded, watered by the Bergh river, and could produce anything and everything, was it tried. Almonds, walnuts, and oranges grow in plenty, but wine is also the chief article here. The 'paint stone' is found in this neighbourhood in quantities— namely, an impalpable powder which, mixed with oil, serves the country people with colour to paint their waggons, houses, etc. This powder is contained within stones of different sizes, and on breaking them the powder comes forth, ground as fine as if it had been done in Bond Street. It is found of all colours but green. We dined at Paarl with a civil, hospitable Dutchman of the name of Alling, the clergyman of the place, and the largest man in height and breadth I ever saw in my life.

We then went on to Waggonmakers' Valley, which is reckoned one of the finest districts in the Colony; but here, or rather on the road here, I still found the same want of trees. Still noble mountains and fine soil, but the human face wanting. We crossed a river by means of a rope and kind of ferry-boat; two men contrived to tow us all over by degrees, the contents of the Landdrost's waggon going first — namely, himself, his wife, three daughters, a slave, Anne, and me; the coachman, waggon, and eight horses followed, which eight horses he drove in hand with as much facility as he would have driven two.

We had arranged to sleep at the house of Mynheer Wegg, which is here pronounced *Veh*. We were received at the door of a very respectable-looking English farm-house by the good people themselves. He was an old soldier with the great King of Prussia,[1] and has therefore a little more of the world about him than most of the other farmers have; his wife is a hale, oldish woman, full of hospitable frankness. But as to size and appearance, suppose John Byng, my friend, near six feet high, and married to Sir Horace Mann, seven feet high and rather more masculine, and then you have both husband and wife. What a happy man Lord

---

[1] Frederick the Great.

Monboddo [1] would be in this country! How it would
corroborate all his doctrines that were we as nature
meant us to be, with no luxury to enervate us, we
should be seven feet at least, or more! Certainly
the *vrow* Veh fell nothing short in her size to
Mynheer Alling, and several Dutch neighbours who
came while we were there, partly from curiosity
and partly to pay their respects to the Landdrost,
were equal to them. We found at Waggonmakers'
Valley, what is universal in this country, a constant
drinking of coffee going forwards. It is to be found
boiling on the table over charcoal all day long.
Wine handed about half a dozen times in the
course of the evening, pipes filled and smoked by
the gentlemen, and the room filled with slaves—a
dozen at least. Here they were particularly clean
and neat. The *vrow* sat like Charity tormented by
a legion of devils, with a black baby in her arms,
one on each knee, and three or four larger ones
round her, smiling benignly on the little mortals, who
seemed very sweet creatures, and devilish only in
their hue. She and her husband have (for a wonder)
no children of their own; so they mean to leave
their slaves free, and to give amongst them all their

---

[1] James Burnett, Lord Monboddo, was a Scottish judge who had
written a work 'Of the Origin and Progress of Language,' in which
he maintained *inter alia* that the ourang-outang was a class of
human species, and that its want of speech was merely accidental.
His theory had many curious points in common with that of
Darwin. He had also an enthusiastic admiration for the ancient
Greeks, and counselled a return to more primitive ideas. His views
were much ridiculed at the time.

fortune. Of course, these people are likely to be well served for life.

We walked in an orange grove Mynheer had planted himself about eighteen years ago, and which is now extremely beneficial, being loaded with fruit; the trees are above thirty feet high, and some of them are nearly as thick of oranges as of leaves. He had sent twenty-seven waggons to the Cape loaded with oranges, in each waggon six thousand, and he had as many more to send. Mr. Barnard pointed out to the master several articles he might cultivate with great advantage on the warm sides of these sheltered mountains, particularly cotton, coffee, and rice. He meant to do so, he said, and knew that it would answer. As to rice, they gave us some to supper much better than any of the Indian rice I have seen, as it was free from the musty taste that has. We had for supper a Cape ham, fat enough, but it was fat hurried on a lean pig; a buck's hind-quarters served up as you would serve a child going to be whipped— it was well larded and good; two fat ducks, a fowl done with currie, rice well boiled, fine peas, stewed beans, cabbage, potatoes, salad with two dozen of hard eggs for garnish, and a dish of egg-pudding which seemed rather too greasy for me to attack it. We had pastry and fruit after, as is the custom here, and plenty of strawberries of the wood sort, but I do not think a strawberry *is* a strawberry without sugar and cream.

We here found the misfortune of the very scanty

accommodation the Cape people have for friends at their houses, as with every possible exertion there was only *one* room for the Landdrost, his wife, and three daughters, and another for Mr. Barnard and me and Anne. I must here set your mind at rest—though we had but one room, we really had two beds; matters were not so bad as to have one only for all *three*! Above Anne's, in the corner, there was a large opening in the roof. I began to congratulate her on its being a trap-door, and that we should see half a dozen Dutchmen swinging her up to the regions above before morning, but we were mistaken. The only harvest drawn up by this hole in the roof is grain or stores, the upper part of the house being used only as a loft or store-room, the Dutch having no idea of converting it (a few people in Cape Town excepted) into any accommodation for their family use; indeed, they would not believe it was possible to do so in Waggonmakers' Valley.

Next morning we were up betimes, and the first thing we were offered was coffee again. For a second time I feared that there was to be no other breakfast, but I soon saw a plentiful one of more coffee, tea, butter, hard eggs, and meat. This over, we went to pay a visit to the *vrow's* brother, Mynheer Latigaas, at his house some few miles distant. This was by much the best planted and romantic situation I had seen. I only regretted that I could not ask the Landdrost to stop his waggon for me to take some views of it; but we had much to do that day without the stop

I should have produced. I never saw so fine or so thick an oak hedge as here. I am told that an oak is almost at its growth in this country in twenty-five or thirty years, and that its wood is inferior to the European oak in consequence. I don't believe it is. Many things are taken for granted; few people give themselves the trouble to make experiments. The fir was reckoned unfit to repair the wharf till necessity forced its use, and it has proved superior and good in its quality. As for an orange grove, that at Mynheer Latigaas' exceeded, or at least came up to, anything my imagination had formed as luxuriant. Mr. Barnard and I measured some of the trees, and found them nine feet round, and were told they were between fifty and sixty feet high; some of the branches were loaded with fruit in clusters, as our plum trees sometimes are, with forty or fifty great oranges, that were as sweet and good as they looked handsome. Little Vandekict, the Landdrost's youngest daughter, seemed rather too busy amongst them—I feared she would do herself harm. 'Oh no!' she said; 'I have only eaten eleven!' You will easily believe there were a few gripes the day after. We went through Mynheer's wine-house, and bespoke some excellent wine, some of which I hope we shall drink together in London. If we can make them leave out their sulphur this year, we will; to me it is not a great fault, as it gives a clean sharpness to the taste which I don't dislike, but it makes traitors of the wines—it makes them *betray* their country, by prejudicing people against them, as I have before mentioned. We found Mynheer Latigaas still taller than his sister 'Sir Horace,' but lean, and his wife broad enough to have made half a dozen wives. He was making an experiment from which I have good hopes of getting a liqueur nice and new for you, extracting brandy from the sweetest ripe oranges. I think it will answer—*nous verrons*.

After strolling about an hour we returned to the Vehs, where we dined, and proceeded back to Paarl, where Mr. Barnard and I remained all night with the Allings, that I might early next morning go up the mountain and take a view from it, and another of the great stones, which as yet I had only seen at a distance. The rest of the party returned to Stellenbosch. We appointed the Landdrost's lightest equipage for next morning (a second-hand carriage from England) to Klapnutch, a military post half-way back, to meet us, intending to ride there. The evening would have been a long one had not a Dutch conversation with Mynheer Alling been worth many lessons to Mr. Barnard, who, I was charmed to find, could make himself so well understood by the honest clergyman that it was twelve o'clock before they separated—about three hours later than their family hour. However, it was Alling's choice, for the benefit of having a little conversation with a well-bred, well-informed, *civil* Englishman, who I fancy is a being the Dutch do not very often meet. The military quartered amongst them have much too contemptuous a way of treating them ; indeed, I often hear things said of the Dutch, before themselves, which nothing could prevent a gentleman taking notice of but a supposed ignorance of the English language, which, however, they often understand well enough to resent deeply, though they say nothing.

This pastor Alling is a singular compound of learning and ignorance, in my opinion, and of curiosity and incredulity. He has a good deal of science such as books, without the intercourse of conversation, can give a man, but some of the simplest things in life are as new to him as if he had not read of them. He asked Mr. Barnard many questions respecting the Dutch, and, supposing there was a general peace, what would be ceded to us *by* them, and what ceded by us *to* them and the French. He particularised a variety of Dutch and French possessions, as far as I could understand him, to which Mr. Barnard constantly replied: 'We have *that*, at present,' or, 'We took that, at such a time.' He seemed astonished, and could scarce believe we had all that Mr. Barnard advanced. At last, 'St. Domingo,' said he, 'and Ceylon.' 'We took both these places and have them *now*,' replied Mr. Barnard. 'What! Ceylon!' cried the other, half angry: 'You are certainly mistaken, *non, non c'est un peu fort!*' in Dutch. I wonder how he could be ignorant of this. On the other hand, he is full of intelligence concerning natural productions of the country, minerals, and fossils, and has a good museum stocked with many curious things—in particular a fine collection of the horns of African animals, some of which he made me take drawings of. I took a sketch of himself, too, which he sat for, as like as possible, but I dare not show it all the same to any of my English friends here, they set up such a halloo, and make such game of it. Mr. Barrow was with Alling some months ago, and he gave him a considerable collection of minerals, and much useful information about the country.

I often wish, when I hear anything new, curious, or useful, that I could divest myself of that portion of false shame which prevents me from taking out a memorandum-book and marking it down while I remember the particulars, which afterwards escape my memory, and the thing sinks into oblivion. But for a woman very ill-informed on most subjects—I might have said on *all* subjects—to give herself the *air* of wisdom, while she knows how superficial she is, by marking down anything that passes in company, I cannot endure it! It is wilfully drawing on a pair of blue stockings she has no right to wear! In this I often put myself in mind of what an old friend used to say to us when children at her feasts : ' My dears, eat as much as you *can*, but pocket nothing.' Was I a man, I would pocket without shame. It becomes at some time or another useful to him, and teaches the mind the good habit of reflecting on what it hears.

Unfortunately for us, next morning was so very, very bad a day, raining so heavily, that it was impossible to stir out, which was a sad disappointment to me. The only good this rain produced—for everything has its fair as well as foul side—was the self-congratulation of the farmers, who now ventured to calculate on the richest harvest, this only being necessary to ensure one. It had another good effect— it swelled a cascade of one hundred feet high, which we had meant to have gone to see, with such a volume of water, that at the distance of some miles it was so evident as to render nearer inspection unnecessary. The rain did not clear up till the middle of the day, and then I durst not spend two or three hours in drawing, as the carriage and horses were waiting for us. I deferred taking these views, therefore, till we could pay another visit to Pastor Alling, who, we were informed, would accept of no money for his hospitality, which we therefore could only repay by six dozen of English porter, since gone to him.

We left him and his wife, promising to return some day, and proceeded on horseback, sending on our servant before to have the carriage ready. In this situation, cantering along, Mr. Barnard fell in love with a horse which a slave rode without shoes or stockings; he described his master to live across the fields at a certain farm. To it therefore we scampered with the confidence of honest people who suppose no harm is to happen to them, though in Africa, and under the guidance of a black man and a stranger. Nor did any harm happen; we reached the farm-house, where I found a bundle of hearty, hospitable Dutch women, who seemed delighted with my visit, and begged us to stay all night with them. But the horse was too dear—60*l*. The carriage now reached us, and into it we stepped, not without being considerably amused to find that it was an ancient *vis-à-vis* of Old Q.'s,[1] which I well knew again, and which has still his coronet upon it. It served our turn, however, very well, while we skirted the lowering mountains which rose above our heads in all sorts of extraordinary shapes, which constitute their beauty to me. But how out of all calculation it seemed to us that we should be driving together amongst the hills in Africa in old Q.'s *vis-à-vis*, with six horses in hand, for the Landdrost's carriage, being light, had only that number, for which he made us an apology. Would the St. James's Street people believe that a Hottentot driver should be able to guide six or eight horses better than they do two? No. We reached Stellenbosch in safety.

[1] The fourth Duke of Queensberry, familiarly known as 'Old Q.,' was celebrated for his connection with the Turf and his many eccentricities and social follies.

'And there, insatiate yet with folly's sport,
That polish'd sin-worn fragment of the Court;
The shade of Queensb'ry should with Clermont meet
Ogling and hobbling down St. James's Street.'

Mr. Barnard was off again to the Cape next day, and returned the day after to accompany us to the Valley of Drakenstein, which is reckoned one of the richest in the whole country. We went by that mountain called Simon's Berg, with its high forked top, where an adventurer some years ago pretended he had found a mine. He melted down a quantity of Spanish dollars into a mass, mixed with a certain quantity of rubbish, to take in the Dutch East India Company, who paid him down a large sum of money to furnish him with the means of returning them a larger. In the meantime they converted the mass of silver into a chain to suspend the keys of the Castle gates, as a proof of their riches, where it still remains, though now a proof of their folly, as the man never found the mine, nor they the money they had lent him to search for more.

We found the road through the Valley of Drakenstein in many places so very bad that we trembled for the Fiscal's cabriole, in which we were on that occasion with the Landdrost, but we got through it safe. The finest mountain that fancy can form is to the left on this road. Had poor Burke, who I fear is no more, seen it, he would have said that when found the Almighty had *riven* it in two, to divide between his countries, but had stopped in the intention when half executed. I do not think it is the Simon's Berg which I allude to, but another mountain whose name I have not yet obtained. This valley is without doubt the richest land and the best in the Colony. Some bulbs that I had pulled up came with a fat soil round them which could have raised better things had it been put to good account. The land is plentifully watered by streams that are never dry. It was extraordinary to us, however, that in all our progress we had not seen buck, hare, nor partridge. There is plenty of game, I am told, a hundred miles or more up the country, but as far as *we* have seen of it, nothing to be compared to England. Game, however, there must be, from the quantity we receive from our friends.

We dined at Herold's farm; the owner was a plain Boer with a large family of children, as they all have. I liked to see the ducks and chickens walk about in the room, as if part of the company, and with pleasure observed two or three swallows' nests in the corners of the room, which I imagine it would be deemed unlucky to pull down, else their love of propriety would make them do so. There were two pretty daughters, who will be so for a year or two more, but then one of the chief features of beauty almost invariably begins to go—namely, the front teeth, which are rarely possessed by the women after thirty; smoking saves the men's, but it leaves them black. I am quite delighted to find that their pipes are no longer offensive to me. I even begin to like the smell of the tobacco, and to wish that, when I sent away all the little furniture from our home to the Government House, to his Excellency, who, poor man, had none, I had reserved a few of the tobacco jars which they use on these occasions. Jesting apart, we have not yet had any smoking in our house, but I see it must be such a want to a Dutchman when he has not his pipe after dinner, that we are going to provide ourselves with some tobacco and pipes for them.

I was pleased with the reception of the Herolds; indeed, I have met with in all the people I have seen on this little tour an open frankness that gave one a share of what they had, apart as I believe from any views beyond the pleasure of bestowing. I think the Boers, or farmers, of the country, as far as I have seen or heard of them, a better charactered race than the people of Cape Town. The first are plain unlettered folks, without emulation and without ambition ; the others are greedy and jealous of each other, but along with this they are equally void of emulation, or of any ambition beyond that of gaining a livelihood out of the chances that arise. No man has any fixed calling, but lives by his wits, and by the purchase of such articles as can be kept, and sold out or bartered to advantage at some future time. Their plans, therefore, and turn of mind are on a very contracted scale. They remind me of the second or third class of mercantile life in England ; this, accompanied with a degree of pride above acknowledging what necessity forces the individual to do, forms an awkward and inconsistent manner. I have not seen in any man or woman of this country one sparkle of what I could suppose was genius, or of any special talent or ability to make one regret that improvement from education should have been wanting. The Fiscal is the pleasantest, and I fancy the best informed and laborious man in Cape Town. His size is immense for his age, which is only thirty-two, but he is not lazy, and has a more gentleman-like turn of mind and a better fund of conversation than the others.

I like the Landdrost of Stellenbosch and his brother-in-law very well too, because they have been kind to us; but the Landdrost is dull—he does not, to quote some lines on Wolfe, ' put so much of his heart into his acts that all must follow that which all approve.' I believe we have been of some use to him in showing him more of his district than he ever saw before. Civility to us has carried him farther than curiosity ever did before, but as he has been Landdrost only two years, he has probably had, as yet, but little time to go about. It is a situation of considerable business, one day with another bringing him on an average not fewer than fifty people, or fifty differences of some sort to settle. But when the Landdrost is a sensible, honest man, how much better this is than to have a breed of lawyers in the country! Though the parties should come at the most inconvenient times, as they often have to come far, he does not keep anyone a moment waiting, but leaves his dinner scarce touched to discuss the affair. An instance of this I shall particularise, because it will make you smile.

The Landdrost was called away the beginning of dinner one day to talk to an old man and old woman who had come together; they detained him long. At last, when he returned, he told us it was an affair of jealousy, founded on what often takes place in this country, the partiality of the master to one of his black slaves; that all was amicably settled, as he had consented to sell the object of contention. He had not had two mouthfuls when another message came from the husband, to the effect that there being a sale in Hottentot Holland next day, he begged leave to sell her then. The Landdrost gave permission, thinking his hurry a proof that the man knew his own weakness, and was resolved to put future error out of his power. Two more mouthfuls were not swallowed, when the wife came back, and off the Landdrost was again. 'Come,' said I, 'I'll lay a rupee on old Sarah's head that she means to be generous, and since her husband is ready to sell the bondwoman to satisfy her, that she is now willing to let her and Ishmael remain.' The gentlemen shook their heads, but no one took my bet, as the appearance was in my favour. At last the Landdrost returned, and we eagerly inquired the old lady's business. 'Only to persuade me to give her leave to whip Hagar,' said he, 'before she is sold.' 'Oh, damn her,' cried Mr. Barnard. 'Amen,' said I, 'but I hope you did not consent?' 'No, no,' said he, ' I thought the concession of selling her quite enough, and refused her revengeful request.'

I since hear that, instead of having sold her, she has brought her to Cape Town and put her into the Fiscal's prison, in hopes of obtaining, from his ignorance of the matter, the general permission to whip her ill-behaved slave. But the Fiscal does not condemn so slightly; he inquired into the merits of the case, and poor Hagar has once more escaped her licking, but is to be sold incontinently.

On Sunday evening we had an impromptu ball at the Landdrost's; the young Dutchmen of the neighbourhood attended—awkward enough youths indeed—and a dozen of young ladies, amongst whom was a lately married Jacobin beauty of the name of Rousseau, of six feet and two inches high, broad in proportion, a Glumdalclitch likeness of the Duchess of Devonshire. Her age is only sixteen, so we may prophesy much for her future greatness! The young women are often good-looking at that age, but they all want softness. When they are, what is supposed here, well educated they have great ideas of keeping up their dignity, and not being put upon, which dignity, being rather coarsely supported, becomes a haughty pride or saucy gaiety as the fair one happens to be grave or merry. I can only quote, by way of instance of the last, the reply of a young lady to an officer who was lamenting that he had not seen her for a long time: 'Well, you see me now, don't you?' There was no harm, to be sure, in the speech, but I felt that if I had been he, I should not have cared whether I ever saw her again! We had some droll minuets at this ball, but I am one of those never known to smile at anybody or anything. I was a simple spectatress. After the dance we had an excellent supper. The thing which amused me most at it was the entrance of two sucking babies, the mothers being of the party and suckling the children themselves. Here we might have venerated the simplicity of the Golden Age, no false delicacy created by luxury stepping in between the cup and the lip to prevent the little ones from having their repast as well as we. While the partners ate and drank heartily, the *clynies*—viz. the *moye kinder* (pretty little children—to translate for you, you European great man)—were busy in their way, to the great discomposure of my liege lord, who drew up his eyebrows and looked at me in despair, having no other place where he could throw his eyes without meeting with what seemed very unfit company for a ball. However, I look on this as of little consequence. 'Tis nonsense to expect the polish of countries that have been refining themselves for ages till they refine themselves away altogether—which is the lot of all worldly things—in one that has not been discovered or inhabited by Christians above one hundred and fifty years. I am in no hurry to send off the *kinder* from the balls. The more the mothers attend to them, and the less they flirt at the Cape with the English officers, so much the better for Mynheer. I believe I told you the speech of Goetz, the late Secretary, to Lord Macartney, when talking of Madame Goetz, his wife : '*Grâce à Dieu ! ma femme est bien laide.*'

After having made a very pleasant expedition we returned to Cape Town. I should gladly have gone farther up the country, but Mr. Barnard could no longer remain absent. Lord Macartney himself means to make a tour of the same sort, but waits the arrival of the next despatches from England very anxiously. Indeed we all long for them from various motives. We have seen old England (well governed) rub through so many hazardous moments, that we hope, alone as she now stands almost, to hear of her doing the same again. But certainly the last accounts of the French success,[1] and the plans against England, which were supposed to be ripe for carrying into execution some months ago, must make us very eager to hear of a satisfactory result. Invasion somewhere I suppose we must expect to hear of. Well! let the worst come! I suppose the worst that can happen will be a bad peace. To make one such, or to see one made, would vex you all as Ministers, while as men, perhaps, you might be contented with a sacrifice of a lump of national glory to private repose and cessation of hostility.

[1] Probably an allusion to Bonaparte's successful campaign in Italy and the attempted invasion of England in conjunction with Spain, which Nelson and Jervis defeated off Cape St. Vincent.

Commissary Pringle told me just now that he had been advertising for a contractor to build chaff-houses, or some sort of public store for such matters as fall within his department. This has thrown the Dutch into great astonishment! '*Mon Dieu*, the English then believe they still are to keep the Cape.' Not one of the Dutch believes it, and even amongst those of the English, who treat everything serious lightly, bets are laid of five to one that the place is ceded on a peace. All the world believe in the peace before Christmas but I, and I hear I am a fool for not believing in one. *Nous verrons*. I can't think that we will consent to all the French require to make a peace. If there is one, and there is still longer use for us here, well, we shall pass our time the more softly that we are on terms of the very best sort with the native Dutch. If there is no more for us to do, we shall see you all again the sooner. Come what will, I shall never regret having visited South Africa. I have seen new scenes, and the able Master Barnard has been initiated in a life of business which has given him that method which will probably on many future occasions render him useful. Certainly it has been of use to him already, by developing powers which had never before been called into action.

I shall not give you in this letter any particular account of your friends here, except by saying that all are well; our soldiers at their camps, our ladies, I hear, gay; but I have been living with country folks, picking up flower roots and opening our eyes wide on the face of Nature instead of opening them on the human form divine adorned with scarlet coats, so I cannot give you more than this general information. By the bye, I should tell you that I hear Mrs. Captain Campbell is in a way of increasing her family; it is so.

I long to send you—indeed it is now on board—a great curiosity—a rump of Cape beef, salted by the Fiscal. '*Oui, mi ledi, par mes propres mains.*' '*Monsieur, les grands hommes sont égaux à tout.*' This, with a mutton ham by Madame the Landdrost, will give you a proper idea of our fare. If they are not good when they arrive it is no fault of mine—I am *sure* they were good when they set off. I also send you a box of ostrich eggs, the freshest I could obtain. I am told by oiling them well and packing them with bran they often keep to reach Holland good; if so, they may reach Wimbledon. There are six eggs, one of them being emptied by me to make some cakes and to try if it was good. Nothing could be more capital than my cakes; make your cook open one in the same manner, and if what it contains is sweet (which I hope it will be), then boil another to be quite hard, which is the way they are here reckoned most delicious, taken *whole* out of the shell and eaten with oil and vinegar; but be sure to have it served up entire, and not cut into pieces. If you will give one of the eggs to my sisters, and one to the Douglas's, or a share of one of them, I shall be much obliged to you. In the same box you will find a candle of my own making, of the vegetable wax (I have not burnt any yet, but I believe it burns dim, as its colour gives one a right to expect), and a small specimen of the syrup of the sugar tree; I could not make the box contain a quart, which I was sorry for. I forgot to put in a specimen of lead ore rough from one of the mountains; I'll enclose a scrap of it only to show you how pure it is found, in large pieces as great as your hand. I am sure there must be many wonderful things hidden in these stupendous hills.

I have not told you, by the bye, that on our return home from Stellenbosch we dined with General Vandeleur at Strickland, and saw for the first time this very barren and cheerless station for the cavalry. There is but a scanty portion of water, and that not good; no pasture or shade for the horses; so there is not any sensible motive for having fixed them there in preference to other and better situations. However, this was before our time.

I think, my dear friend, I ought here to make you common-sense apology for the many vague things I say and repeat. I never mean to be unjust or erroneous, but ignorance may often make me so, for which reason I confine myself more to the subject of things than of people, as the first cannot be equally injured by any misapprehension of mine. Wise and worldly people are always afraid of committing to paper opinions respecting anything

beyond the merest trifles, unless they foresee events.
I, for instance, was I to treat you like a Minister
instead of a man and a friend, would not send you
off my details of the Cape, nor say what I think of it,
till I knew whether it was to be kept by us or not. In
the last case it would be flattering to speak highly
in its praise, in the first to hold it light; but this is
not a fit way of dealing between you and me. I
must therefore conclude by saying that I hope it
will be found possible to keep the Cape; that barren
and ill-cultivated as it now is, it strikes both Mr.
Barnard and me to have great powers in itself to
become one of the finest countries in the world.
How far it will be the wisdom of England to encourage it to become so is for England's Sovereign
and his Ministers to determine. Whether it will be
more for England's advantage, and that of our possessions in India, to keep it subordinate, so that it may
never interfere, while it aids and assists the to-and-fro constantly going on between England and India,
is for you to determine, and you only. The choice
climate and fertile soil here might certainly make it
a second India, but whether in that point of view
Ceylon might not be a better *pis aller*, supposing
anything to go wrong with us in the East, is a point
I have heard questioned. If the world was at peace,
and was I a monarch, I should like to portion a
younger son with the Cape, supposing him little,
for a ten years' minority would produce a vast
difference in this country, if it was as much

encouraged as it has been repressed. Yet it is possible (if we keep it) that you may be obliged from policy to adhere to the same selfish considerations which governed the Dutch. The most enlightened of the inhabitants complain of the late *régime*. Their hands were tied up from being possessed of the riches they might so easily have enjoyed from their industry. They tell me there is nothing this place is not equal to, particularly if we can suppose the intercourse between the inner parts of the country and Cape Town rendered more easy. It is certainly a healthy climate.

VII

The Castle, Cape of Good Hope:
February 3rd, 1798.

I CANNOT let the 'Buccleugh' sail, my dearest Friend, without a cordial line expressive of the happiness I feel on this great and gallant victory of Admiral Duncan's.[1] Added to many other powerful motives for rejoicing, the exultation which *you* would feel at the manner in which your favourite has distinguished himself, and the transport of his wife and family, come in for their share. She is my old acquaintance, though it is a thousand years since we saw each other. Tell the Admiral that the ballad written on his victory and conduct on that day, and repeated to me by Lord Mornington, had the same effect on me as Lord Lansdowne had on the present Lady Campden, 'it made me all over goose-skin.' But it went farther: it made me greet the triumph with a few salt, yet sweet, tears, such as the geese called women sometimes shed on such occasions. I wish we had oftener cause.

[1] The battle of Camperdown—Admiral Duncan's victory over the French fleet under Admiral de Winter (October 11, 1797). For this victory Admiral Duncan was made Viscount Duncan of Camperdown.

I do not mean to encroach much on your time at present, as you will hear everything worth knowing from a quarter so much superior, Lord Mornington.[1] He and his brother,[2] with Sir Hugh Christian,[3] arrived here on the 28th of January, both well, and greatly enjoying dry land after their voyage. We had got ready a comfortable suite of apartments for Lord Mornington, and pressed him to accept of it, till we perceived that our *own Lord* rather wished him to reside in one of the houses that admit of lodgers here, from an unwillingness, I think, to see him accommodated in any other house connected with the Government than his own. Yet in his own Lord Mornington could not have been, as Lord Macartney has only furnished what is necessary for his household. Fortunately for us, and for Lord Mornington too I think, he was attacked by *bugs* in the abode he went to, which settled the matter and

[1] The Earl of Mornington, afterwards Marquess Wellesley, who had been appointed Governor-General of India. He stopped at the Cape for some time on his way out to India to see Lord Macartney, who had at one time been Governor of Madras, and to meet Lord Hobart, who was returning home from India, after having been Governor of Madras. The result of their consultation at the Cape was that Lord Mornington resolved to restore our power in India to the same footing as it had stood at the peace of Seringapatam. In this he was acting also on the wishes of the President of the Board of Control, Henry Dundas.

[2] The Hon. Henry Wellesley, afterwards Lord Cowley. Colonel Arthur Wellesley was another brother, afterwards Duke of Wellington.

[3] Rear-Admiral Sir Hugh Christian was sent out to the Cape as second in command of the fleet there; he succeeded Admiral Pringle as Commander-in-Chief in April 1798, but died suddenly a few months later, in November 1798.

put it fully in his power to say to us: 'Pray, pray, as you offered to take me, do.' Here he came, and is, the pleasantest companion and easiest guest, as is his brother too, who, though sick at sea, is now perfectly well. As to Lord Mornington, he is as well, or better than I ever saw him—eats heartily of anything and everything, and says he takes many liberties with the 'Governor-General' he never before dared to take with Lord Mornington, and finds no bad effects from them. He is much charmed with Lord Macartney's manners. He finds them more pleasing in some respects than he looked for; ability and knowledge he expected, but there is a mildness and consideration of everybody, with a sort of parental affection to those immediately attached to him, which he did not expect in the degree he finds it. Wines of strong body and high flavour are sometimes ameliorated by time, and become more gracious to the taste than when new! We have dined twice with Lord Macartney, and to-day he dines with us, and also generals, colonels, admirals, and twenty-two of the great men of the Cape; so I, being a little in the Martha way, thinking of many things, though not troubled about any, will bid you adieu for the present. In a few days we shall give a ball, when everybody will have the opportunity of paying their respects to the Governor-General of India. The Governor once thought of giving one, but there was no means, the fair Scold of the great ball-room having lost her husband ten days ago, and being now wedded to a Dutch officer, who thinks it beneath his dignity to permit any more balls.

This day the 'Belvidere' arrived, and I have seen Mr. Holland,[1] who has been anxiously expected for some time past to judge on prizes, in their nature doubtful. He seemed surprised that anyone should look for him with anxiety, as he had supposed he should be quite an idle man. The more he has to do the better.

Lord Mornington expects to be able to proceed on his voyage in a week, and while necessary repairs are putting the ship in order he is having some accommodations put up for himself, which, however, he swears he will sail without if the other business of the ship can be finished sooner than this can. He little knows how unlikely it is for any ship that touches here to get off in ten days, if there is but a nail to put in, or a cask of water to be shipped. If he is off in three weeks, I shall say his captain has made more haste than any other my twelve months' experience of them has shown me. However, as his ship will in many respects be improved and lightened, she will sail the faster for the present delay, and certainly the more securely, as she was dangerously overmasted before the masts were cut lower. By

[1] Mr. John Holland was appointed Postmaster-General with an office in the Castle. This was the first Post Office at the Cape, and the revenue brought in about 200*l.* per annum.

the time of his departure we expect the Anstruthers will arrive.

When they leave us, we shall endeavour to get to our cottage in the country for a couple of months, February and March being hot months in town. As yet we have felt no inconvenience in the Castle from the heat of the weather, flies, or mosquitoes; indeed, all has been comfortable to us, and we have been as happy as people can be at a distance from some of those they love best. The object of our being here is fully answered, and that to me is the great point. I trust that Mr. Barnard has filled the situation well that you placed him in, and acquired under his skilful and kind master that method in the transaction of business which will render him on future occasions useful. My kind love to Lady Jane; tell her that Lord Mornington expresses himself often of her in terms so high, and at the same time so affectionate, that I have wished her more than once behind the curtain. I might safely wish her this in *our* drawing-room, which has French ones. But in any of the Dutch drawing-rooms she would be discovered, as all the curtains are Highlanders, their kilts reaching only half-way to the ground.

February 16*th*.—My letter was too late for the 'Buccleugh,' and so I am adding to it. My prophecies have been right. We have still our friends with us, and I declare that we shall see them depart with great sorrow. They expect, however, to go on board the day after to-morrow, and I believe them when they tell me that they shall be equally sorry to bid adieu to us, as they have both amused themselves in a quiet way extremely, picking up a little fun out of everything, yet laughing at none of our grandees. As to Lord Mornington, if ever I saw a man the purity of whose conduct under any temptation (I mean of the Oriental sort) I could count on, I think it is he. His whole soul seems turned to do his duty well—his pride, his pleasure, the anticipation of approbation from you all at home and of his own conscience. Added to this there is the certainty that, from the savings of his large income, he must make a handsome provision for his younger children, a duty in his situation which I do believe he will fulfil in its fair and honourable extent.

Having talked over such views lately in the confidence of mutual good opinion, you may judge how I was entertained last night when I saw offered to him what I called his 'first bribe.' His Excellency the Governor of Mozambique, a stately well-stuffed Portuguese, full of dignity and grave folly, supped here last night with our two Excellencies. He had to attend him a black dwarf, of about thirty-four inches high, dressed in uniform. He was a fool, but the Governor said he had *beaucoup d'esprit*, which gave us no high idea of *his*. While at cards he was in a great fuss, when supper was announced, lest all the first places should be taken before his rubber was over—not having at all supposed it possible that the other two Governors and the mistress of the house should wander about *sans façon* while the company seated themselves. Fortunately a place at the very upper end remained vacant, in which he placed himself, and did great honour to the provisions before him. When the company, all but a few, rose, Lord Mornington and I sat down next him. Lord Mornington, for conversation, praised a cane which he carried, of very fine workmanship in gold—gold ribbon, head, tassels, etc.—quite a presentation thing. It was immediately offered to him by the gallant Portuguese, and declined with a very disconcerted air by Lord Mornington, who had not been aware what his compliment was to produce. Again it was offered, pressed, insisted on. He had *plusieurs des autres*; '*mi lor Signor*' must do him the honour to accept of the *bagatelle*. At last Lord Mornington, vexed and almost angry, assured him that *les Anglais* were *si gauche* that they did not know the use of a cane, and never carried one. We laughed a good deal at Lord Mornington for having been so publicly attacked by a golden fee, and it all passed over mighty well till next day, when, Lord Mornington happening to mention to somebody the *politesse* of the Portuguese Governor, a person more *gauche* than the *Anglais* in general, said he had been told that his Lordship had accepted the cane. This led on to the person's repeating the conversation which one of the people at table during the transaction had held with him, a man who might have known better. Never saw I anybody so angry, so vexed, so provoked as Lord Mornington, 'He may be an excellent *Judge*,' said he, ' but he is d——d bad evidence, when he can so grossly mistake the fact his eyes witnessed.' In spite of his being out of all patience, however, he could not help laughing with Anne Barnard and me at the hopeful paragraph this might make in the newspapers for his friends at home to read from the Cape, that the new Governor of Bengal had not even postponed until his arrival in India his taste for *douceurs*, having accepted a cane set with jewels value 5,000 dollars from the Governor of Mozambique. Trifling as this appeared to be to us, who had seen it all, it has been deemed worthy of a few words to the narrator to put him right as to the fact. Don't suppose from my having mentioned the word 'judge' that it was our friend Sir John Anstruther,[1] but look amongst our Cape Department, and the head of a certain Board, for the *mal entendu*. It fidgeted Lord Mornington for a day and a-half, more than you can well imagine.

Within these two or three days, various ships are come in; in particular one from Bengal loaded with Generals—Duff, Jones, and Morgan. The last named

[1] Sir John Anstruther was an Indian judge, Chief Justice of Bengal. He had probably come to the Cape to meet Lord Mornington.

is plainly made of teak-wood, which is so hard and firm, you know, as to endure time and be insensible to decay. Many other Indian officials of some ability are residing here, so we have a Bengal *levée* every morning at breakfast, the individuals of which are closeted and pour the riches of their knowledge and experience on Lord Mornington, who seems anxious to gain all he can from them. Sir Hugh Christian I like much; he appears to be a mild, firm, intelligent man, and a pleasing companion. I expect satisfaction from his society.

Admiral Pringle is certainly very clever and entertaining; Lord Mornington is delighted with him in the midst of all his singularity. But he is too great a growler. 'Well, and how do *you* like the Cape, my Lord?' said he to Lord Mornington. 'Upon my word, sir, I like it very much.' 'Ay, ay, you would say that after such a voyage as yours, if you had landed in hell.' He says Lord Macartney understands a table no more than a whale, which is a good seafaring simile for a great man. Yet, with all this, I do *not* think that he likes to go, and shrewdly suspect he would not have been displeased had a little *douce* violence been used to make him stay *malgré lui*. At present 'tis an awkward situation for sweet Sir Hugh to be in, but he says nothing, though I can see he feels himself out of his place. I hear, about a fortnight hence Admiral Pringle will be going home, but I cannot help thinking it may be longer, if he waits the return of a cruising expedition which some time ago took away some of our ships. Added to other motives which may detain him a little, almighty love may have its share, perhaps, though it is said that that god has already engaged him to a lady in England, now lying at anchor to wait his return. He and Sir Hugh dined here yesterday, Lord Mornington and his brother, the Anstruthers, and a couple of Navy captains—a snug, small party. It quite delights me to hear a little pleasant talk. Things ran rather more than was quite agreeable in the flirting line at one time here, but the minority—namely, Anne Barnard and I—have received great additions by the arrival of Mrs. Holland, the Morningtons, Sir Hugh Christian, etc., and hope to be able to make time amble very agreeably without drinking, gaming, or making love. I own these three auxiliaries give the strongest zest of any to society, but all three are intoxications which produce mischief to heads and hearts. God bless you.

VIII

The Castle, Cape of Good Hope:
June 6th, 1798.

THE enclosed journal, my dear Friend, will give you, I hope, some idea of the tour which I have made into the interior of the country since you last heard from me. I have put it in this form, as you will then be able to go over the ground with me, at least, in your imagination. The month of May is not the month of flowers here, as it is at home; on the contrary, it is at the Cape our November, and the beginning of the rainy season. After having sent off the Governor-General to India in good health, resolved like Sancho Panza to be an upright Governor, we went to Paradise, where we meant to have remained for a month or two without a break, and had requested the Anstruthers to come to us, but the gout prevented him, and a considerable taste for the pleasures of the Cape seemed to prevent her. Then Lord Macartney told Mr. Barnard that if he wished to see a little of the country, and did not think it too late, he might go for a month, as there was then no business which could not be transacted in his absence. But, he added, it was possible that at the end of that time he (Lord Macartney) might be receiving despatches from England which would give him leave to depart in two or three months, and then he could not do without Mr. Barnard, still less could any successor spare him who might be new to the business of the Colony. On these considerations, and the possibility of a peace, and of the Cape being given up—unlikely enough, but within the chapter of chances—we thought it best, as it were, to catch Time by the forelock and set off. The prospect of a holiday to a poor secretary who had been screwed down to his desk for a twelvemonth was an offer much too welcome not to be accepted.

Our young cousin Jane preferred accompanying us to remaining at the Castle, and as a young lady, like a great general, is nothing without a proper staff, Mr. Barnard invited my cousin John Dalrymple to be her *aide-de-camp*. Johnny is somewhere from five to seven feet high; as he grows an inch or two every fortnight, there is no knowing where to fix him. As a cornet he is fond of his gun, but fonder of his horse, and the prospect of being jolted in a waggon over some hundreds of miles with the beauty of the garrison, to the exclusion of all the generals, colonels, and field officers, filled him with rapture. We had with us also Mr. Barnard's servant, Pawell, the Brabanter, master of French, English, and Dutch, who is active, young, and fond of excursions.

So much for the company, now for the conveyance. Of course, it was a Cape waggon; any other sort of carriage in this country it is impossible to think of for such an excursion. An ox waggon would have suited our pockets best, being exactly half the price of a horse one; but it goes very slowly, and as a month was all we could possibly afford, we could not cover half as much ground in the time. So we determined on horses, though we knew we should have to hire oxen also occasionally to take us over the *kloofs*, or steep passes in the mountains. The hire of our waggon, coachman, and eight horses, came to about three guineas a day. The waggon was long and narrow, after the fashion of those here, and had over it a stout sailcloth cover, very necessary in this climate. We then set to to add what was necessary to make our month as comfortable as might be. This, as a careful *haus-vrow*, devolved on me. To begin with, I had a couple of sailcloth bags made to hold a pair of mattresses, two pairs of blankets, sheets, pillows, etc., in case we should find no beds at some of our nightly quarters, or perhaps very dirty ones at that. I also packed up some dozens of handkerchiefs to give to slaves and Boer servants, some ribbands, gold lace, needles, thread, scissors, tea, coffee, sugar, for the Boers themselves, etc., where people would not take money, a lot of pretty coloured beads for Hottentots, and some white pearl beads, some dozens of common knives, a large bale of tobacco, a bundle of candles, different things to eat, and a little bag of *schellings*, or bank notes of sixpence each, in my pocket. To these stores Mr. Barnard added two good hams, a large piece of beef, and two tongues, also a small cask of good madeira, a box of gin, rum, and liquors, and plenty of powder and shot. We also each packed a box containing our special things, over which the seats were hung. By the time this was done we were all ready to start.

Saturday, May 5th, 1798.—Behold us setting out in our waggon and eight at nine o'clock in the morning. On the front seat sat our coachman, Gaspar, lent us by a friend for the journey, an enthroned lord sitting on his own box, which was chiefly filled with tools, nails, and other things which might be useful for purposes of repair. Behind him sat your friend Lady Anne, on her knee an old drawing-book, which little thought in its old age it would be caught turning over a new leaf in the wilds of Africa. By her was her *mann* Mynheer Barnard, with his gun ready to pop at the partridges the minute they appeared. Behind him, seated on the woolsacks—in other words, the mattresses—were cousins Johnny and Jane. Behind this happy pair was Charley, my little black boy, who was appointed inspector of the baggage, ready to holloa out when anything dropped. By him was Hector, a stupid old slave belonging to the coachman, who played the part of a sort of groom and odd man. Behind our waggon followed Pawell and another slave, who rode Mr. Barnard's horse and

Jane's stud—viz. a couple of riding-horses—and a Hottentot riding Johnny Dalrymple's 'Hobgoblin.' These brought up the rear, and you will see made quite an imposing procession.

We left Cape Town by the same road by which we went to Stellenbosch, which is the only egress. Until we passed Rondebosch the road was sandy and heavy, and we proceeded without incident. Mr. Barnard and Johnny had a shot at two bucks, but they escaped, and the only things which fell to their guns were two pheasants and a wild turkey. I saw no tillage till we arrived at Mynheer Meybrough's farm, a well-to-do Dutchman, where we hoped to bed and dine, having come about twenty miles in five hours. We found that he had gone to the Cape, but his *vrow* was at home, a typical Dutchwoman. She gave us an excellent dinner; and though at first I thought she was sulky, it turned out to be only her manner; she was really very hospitable, and glad to see us. Her daughter brought me her child, which was still sucking, and eleven months old. I tried to nurse it, but, alas! could not contain it in my arms, it was such a porpoise. 'What would *mi ledi* give to have such a one?' she asked with maternal pride. I thought if I had, like Solomon, I should be tempted to make two of it. This is one of the great points of vanity with the Dutch, the size and number of their children. I have determined, as I before mentioned, to take the credit of three or four, to ensure for myself proper respect; they must all be left in England, and all boys. I will not enact the girls' mother and leave my girls behind. While we dined, the horses refreshed themselves—that is to say, they had liberty to roll in the sand with all their hoofs in the air, except one hoof, which is tied to the bridle to prevent them escaping; and even to this restraint Cape horses get so accustomed by habit, that I often see them cantering off on three legs as nimbly as a dog. We left these good people at four o'clock, and after another four hours' journey we arrived at the next Mynheer's, where we understood we were to be accommodated for the night. Alas! we found them all gone off on a visit, even the children and most of the slaves, but they had left behind them the tutor, who received us, and we made the best shift we could.

Sunday, May 6th, 1798.—After making a tolerable breakfast from our own tea, just with the addition of some fresh eggs, which we bought, we started. We hired a team of oxen to carry us to the foot of the Hottentot Kloof, which we reached in about an hour, having passed but one farmhouse by the way, and not a single tree or bush. At the bottom of the ascent we found a Boer ready with twelve splendid oxen ready to be put to the waggon. They seemed to dislike the business they were going on, and lowed piteously when they found themselves in the yoke. The ascent is about two miles; for the first mile, wherever the eye turned there was heath, sand, sea, mountain, scarce a house to be seen, no cultivation, and, of course, no population. As we looked back over the wide prospect we were leaving, bay succeeded bay, and hill hill, carrying on the eye over a scene of infinite beauty. The path was very perpendicular, and the jutting rocks over which the waggon was to be pulled were so large that we were astonished how they were accomplished at all, particularly at one part called 'The Porch.' At length we reached the summit, and the new Canaan opened to my eye; hillock upon hillock, mountain behind mountain, as far as the eye could reach, a slight thread of rivulet here and there winding through the valleys like a silver eel. Our descent was much easier accomplished. We went down on foot, and when we got to the bottom we found the waggon safe, and the horses put to it again. I was horrified to see how much the poor oxen had suffered in our service; their sides were streaming down with blood which the knives of the savage drivers had brought forth. They are very cruel here to their cattle—the whip is an implement of torture, and is sometimes supplemented by knives; the drivers are sufficiently good anatomists to know exactly the vital parts to be avoided. We travelled on over a tract of country still innocent of the plough, passing by three rivers, or *rivières*, as they are called here, of which the Palmite was the greatest. Then along a dangerous pass, which with a high loaded waggon and eight horses in hand was not very pleasant, but

M

our driver was extraordinarily skilful. We at last reached the farmhouse where we were to stop for the night. The name of the farmer was Jacob Joubert, a mere Boer; his wife received us—a plain, stupid, but civil woman, strange to say without any children. We made a good dinner with them of some boiled fowls, with plenty of potatoes and butter—a repast fit for an emperor.

Monday, May 7th, 1798.—We started at seven o'clock in the morning, the weather glorious, and all our animals well. We had to engage a further team of twelve oxen to carry us over Howe-hook, another tremendous hill. These cattle were so strong that they pulled us with ease up perpendicular ascents, which made me think that they would pull us like Elijah up to heaven. The vegetation, of tender green and olive and brown, was fresher than the day before. The rocks appeared to be of a bastard white marble, but they said they were limestone; and a lot of the most brilliant everlasting flowers, pinked with black hearts, grew among the heath. The descent was two miles, and before us opened a wide desert, pathless, untenanted; one little bit of smoke only ascended to heaven—it looked like the fire-offering of Cain. Probably it was the fire of some poor Hottentot cooking his humble mess. We now got on to what is called 'The Great Road,' tolerably well beaten by waggons. We were going on to a Mynheer Brandt's, where we intended to pass the night; but we stopped halfway at a farmhouse to rest the horses and have something to eat. I was very tired, and I thought the *stoep* in front of the house the pleasantest of all seats. We made the best meal we could, having as a table the top of an old barrel.

I wanted to stay here all night, but the coachman said that he could go on and reach our destination before sunset. He was mistaken, for after we had gone some time the sun set with a vengeance. There is hardly any twilight here, and in this case there happened to be no moon, so within a quarter of an hour we were plunged from light into total darkness. The road was very rough, and though I made Hector walk at the head of the horses to be doubly sure, suddenly the waggon began to rock. 'Sit tight,' shouted Mr. Barnard. I felt the wheel sinking on the side I was, and, in a moment, down we came like a mountain. The waggon was overturned, my head lower than my heels, and everything in the world, it seemed, was above me. Cousin Jane, Johnny, and I were laid low; Mr. Barnard escaped, and rushed to see how we were. I felt half suffocated with the luggage, and my arm seemed broken, but presently, when they had unpacked me, I crawled out safe on the heath. Presently Jane also emerged, and there we were, bruised, but with no bones broken; it was really a miraculous escape. While they were trying to get the waggon straight again, though they had great fear of doing it, I walked about to discover in the darkness where we were, while Jane sat on a stone, a statue of patience, condoling with herself for the bruises on a white marble arm, the rest of her being preserved, in a most literal sense of the word, for a cask of ginger had had its topknot knocked off in the fall, and had poured its contents in at Jane's neck and out at her toe, by which means she was a complete confection. I could not help laughing, and sat down to count my bruises with her, when we were startled by hearing a voice in the darkness behind us saying, 'Well, to be sure, this is the devil's own circumstance.' I found it proceeded from Cousin Johnny, who had embarked the whole of his fortune, amounting to thirty dollars, in Jane's netting case, which happened to be the only thing lost in our tumble. We all crept after it on our hands and knees in the darkness, but nowhere was it to be found, nor had we a tinder-box to strike a light. 'Well,' said he, with a cornet's philosophy, 'here's for a light heart and a thin pair of breeches,' and he kicked out his foot to emphasise his words, and lo and behold! it struck against something which jingled. I leave you to imagine his transports. Everything was replaced in about an hour, and off we started. But fresh perils awaited us, for we had to cross the river; fortunately the ford was marked out by a stick or two, and we got over it safely. Never was anything so welcome as Mynheer Brandt's house. We entered through a kitchen filled with slaves, many of them with very little covering on. Under the guidance of Gaspar, who turned out to be a man of many talents, we made a most excellent supper, with a little hot wine and water to crown it. Decent beds rendered no trouble in unpacking necessary.

Tuesday, May 8th, 1798.—We had an excellent sleep in one of the tallest beds I ever saw, and a good breakfast; all our bruises tolerable; white marble arm to-day had become *verde antique*, which I tried to convince Jane was a more valuable article. We started off at eight o'clock in the morning, and our road was much the same as other days. There was more game, and we passed through a good deal of low brushwood. At last in the distance appeared stupendous hills of white sand, over which we had to cross; the hills looked as though they were covered with snow, while the air had all the charm of summer without its oppressive heat. Many tremendous mounds of sand did we ascend and descend, our wheels above the axle-trees, and at last we reached a curious cave of petrifactions, called the Drup Kelder—or rather we arrived in the neighbourhood of it, for it took us some time to discover the path, which was steep and dangerous, and had to be done on foot. Sometimes this path was only two feet broad, with a precipice at the side, in which I must assuredly have been dashed to atoms had I fallen; no ascent to the Table Mountain was equal to the dangers and horrors of this. At the cave's mouth there lay sundry bones, but we could not judge what animal they belonged to. Tigers often infest it, and feast on what they drag inside; it was, therefore, necessary to fire a gun before we entered the cavern, and to have plenty of light to intimidate the creatures. Unless in greatest want no savage animals will attack a man; the guides remarked by the trembling of the horses that they smelt tigers near about, but we saw none. We had fortunately brought a tinder-box, and the gloom of the cave was soon illuminated by some wax candles which I packed up after my last party in Berkeley Square — you will remember! They little thought, those candles, when their tops had the honour of shining upon some of their Royal Highnesses, and in your right honourable face, that their bottoms would next illuminate the Drup Kelder in South Africa. The pointed drup stones of stalactites hung down from the roof in great numbers, and sometimes met others which had risen from the ground; it was a curious sight. I am sorry the time did not admit of my drawing it properly. This was our day's excursion, and we did not get back again until eleven o'clock. Mr. Barnard was unwell, and went to bed. I made a fricassee with the 'conjurer,' and very good it was.

Thursday, May 10*th*, 1798.—Nothing of much interest happened yesterday. We journeyed over a barren country, no tillage and no trees, and arrived about six at Mynheer Woolfram's, who runs the Government Baths, where people go for a variety of complaints, and slept there. The next morning, while they were making breakfast ready, I made acquaintance with a pair of young ostriches—the first I have ever seen in my life. They were something so different in their appearance to anything I had ever seen, that, when I perceived a couple of creatures coming towards me, whose long throats reached about four feet higher than the horses' backs, I rubbed my eyes, thinking my head was giddy. After breakfast we went over the Baths; the Government House consists of three or four rooms. The water is introduced in its own stream into a small house where there is a bathing place; it is hot. In the kitchen I admired a very picturesque group—a Hottentot woman in her ornaments, a Boer, little Charley, and slaves, all collected together. The Boer's figure, serenely smoking his pipe, first looking at the Hottentot he was accustomed to see, and then at the Englishwoman he had never seen before, was a picture.

We set off again in our waggon, favoured with another charming day. Our object this morning was to see those humble missionaries who, sent by the Moravian Church about seven years ago, have made so great a progress in converting the Hottentots to Christianity. I had heard much of them, and I desired with my own eyes to see what sort of people Hottentots are when collected together in such an extensive *kraal* as that which surrounds the settlements of the fathers. Hitherto I had only seen the servants of the farmers kept to hard work and humiliating subjection. We travelled on over rough ground, and after about four hours arrived at the base of the Baviaan and Boscheman's Kloofs, where the settlement was. Each step we now took we found a bit of grass or a few cattle, a *kraal* or a hut, a cornfield, a little garden, and a general look of peace and prosperity, which seemed to me the tacit manna of the Almighty showered down upon His children. The fathers, of whom there were three, came out to meet us in their working jackets, each man being employed in following the business of his original profession—miller, smith, carpenter, and tailor in one. They welcomed us simply and frankly, and led us into their house, which was built with their own hands five years ago. They told us that they were sent by the Moravian Church in Germany; that their object was to convert the Hottentots and render them industrious, religious, and happy; that they had spent some time in looking out for a proper situation, sheltered, of a good soil, and near water; that they had found it here, and had procured some Hottentots to assist them in the beginning of the work, and by their treatment of them had gradually encouraged more to creep around them. 'This gate,' said one of the fathers, 'and all the ironwork is my *broeder's* making.' The other two had raised the walls, which were of clay mixed with stone. The tailor had taught the Hottentot women to make rush mats of a sort of reed, with which the floor of the church was covered. They asked us to step in to see the church; we found it about forty feet long and twenty broad; the pulpit was a platform raised only a few steps above the ground, and matted with some rushes, on which were three chairs and a small table, on which was a Bible. I regretted very much that it was not Sunday—then I should have found the whole community, about three hundred Hottentots, assembled to Divine worship. The fathers said I should still see them, as at sunset every day, when business was over, there were prayers. Presently the church bell was a-ringing, and we begged leave to make part of the congregation. I doubt much whether I should have entered St. Peter's at Rome, with the triple crown, with a more devout impression of the Deity and His presence than I felt in this little church of a few feet square, where the simple disciples of Christianity, dressed in the skins of animals, knew no purple or fine linen, no pride or hypocrisy. I felt as if I was creeping back seventeen hundred years, and heard from the rude and inspired lips of Evangelists the simple sacred words of wisdom and purity. The service began with a Presbyterian form of psalm; about one hundred and fifty Hottentots joined in the twenty-third psalm in a tone so sweet and loud, so chaste and true, that it was impossible to hear it without being surprised. The fathers, who were the sole music-masters, sang in their deep-toned bass along with them, and the harmony was excellent. This over, the miller took a portion of the Scripture and expounded it as he went along. The father's discourse was short, and the tone of his voice was even and natural, and when he used the words, as he often did, *myne lieve vriende*, 'my beloved friends,' I felt that he thought they were all his children.

We made a most excellent supper, and the fathers ate with us. I must say they had excellent appetites—they urged one another on. 'Broeder, eat this,' and 'Broeder, take another slice,' and 'Ledi, ask him, he likes it.' This was *à propos* of one of our cold hams, for they had not tasted one since they left Germany, they said. So, of course, we left what remained of it for them. Our cask of madeira and our gin were next produced, and they gladly partook of it, as it was a day of *fête*. They had accustomed themselves to do quite without wine, and even without meat, living on the simplest fare. Their position, they told us, was one of great danger, for the Boers disliked them for having taken the Hottentots away from the necessity of laborious servitude, and 'over and over again,' they told us, 'the farmers had made plots to murder us. The last plot, which was to shoot us with poisoned arrows, we discovered and were able to prevent.' Mr. Barnard was very much interested in this, and promised to speak to the Governor to see what was best to be done for their security. We spent the night in a small sitting-room on a couple of cane sofas very comfortably.

Friday, May 11*th*, 1798.—We rose betimes next morning, and three hours before we started. We were to get to Sweet Milk Valley that evening—a military quarter for the cavalry, and reckoned the most beautiful situation in the country. I spent these three hours inspecting the garden, with which I was greatly pleased, and then went out to see the Hottentots working in a field. They seemed to be very cheerful and well-to-do. I also went into the smith's workshop, and found two or three Hottentots at work making knives, which was very ingenious of them; in fact, the more one saw of this settlement the more one found to admire in it. Our drive this day was uneventful, and we arrived at Sweet Milk Valley in the evening.

Saturday, May 12*th*, 1798.—The Sweet Milk Valley did not come up to my expectations. I was told of charming woods, where the greatest variety of choice timber was to be found, ebony or blackwood, satinwood, and the wild olive, which resembles tortoiseshell when polished; but I found not a tree. I learnt afterwards that there was a deep glen between the rising ground and the mountains, but we did not see it. We travelled on to the Landdrost's of Swellendam, and to our dismay found that he was at the Cape, and, what was worse, he had locked everything up. So we made shift in an outhouse.

Sunday, May 13*th*, 1798.—Woke up very early, after a good nap, but could not help laughing very heartily, we resembled so much a set of strolling players in a barn. I prepared a very excellent breakfast for my fellow actors, and thieved a few feathers out of a wing of a flamingo for my sisters. We departed with a guide, and saw but one house for five miles, and that another Landdrost's, with *kraals* of Hottentots all round it, belonging to the farm, all naked.

Our gentlemen had a good deal of sport to-day. First Johnny shot a pow (a wild peacock), a very fine bird, with grave colours, but rich brown; then three ostriches appeared in the distance and a secretary bird, and Mr. Barnard wanted to shoot him, but Gaspar shook his head and cried, '*Neit goed! Neit goed!*' It seems to be very unlucky to kill one, besides being contrary to law, as they are supposed to destroy certain enormous snakes. Corehens, partridges, and curlew also fell to our guns. We dined to-day *al fresco* on the ground, with a good deal of thorn growing all about us. The thorn I found is called the cuckold tree, from the horns it bears, and, being all white, at a distance it looks like a tree covered with snow. After dinner we drove twenty miles without seeing a house, cornfield, or human creature, and at last arrived at the house of Jacob van Rhenin. It was pitch dark when we got there. We were met at the door by Jacob and his *vrow* and a whole 'clutch' of fair children, and many black. The house was of the ordinary Dutch style of architecture, but rather better in some respects, with more rooms, certainly more comfortable. The *vrow* was of the same size and age as all the married women of the Colony; they bear half a dozen children to begin with, and as soon as they have done that, they put on five-and-thirty stone as a matter of course. They have no idea of continuing to look handsome to please their husbands. A blue stuff petticoat, a cotton bed-gown with long sleeves, a shawl, handkerchief, and round pleated morning cape is the dress of every woman at the Cape when at home. The *vrow* was very cheerful, kindly, and accommodating. She pointed to the fire, where tea and coffee boiled over charcoal all day long, and milk the same, saying: 'Mak self, know best vat like,' which seemed to me very sensible. We did ample justice to a very good supper. The *vrow's* father, a very old and beautiful figure, supped in his nightcap with us, as did Jacob. A Dutchman is never happy until he gets his cap and nightgown and his pipe.

Monday, May 14th, 1798.—We made a long expedition to-day to shoot game. Gaspar drove, and Jacob manipulated the whip, which he applied with such effect to the eight horses that they set off at full gallop, leaving the winds behind them. Game bolted out on all sides—ostriches, pows, young ducks, wild geese, steinbocks, bontebocks, and roebucks. But what will you think of our sportsmen? Not one was shot! We got back in time for dinner, and had a fine dish of oysters by way of a treat. Our host proposed next day a fishing expedition to Bredde River. He went there twice a week in fine weather, 'and my fat woman,' taking his wife by the hand, 'will have no objection to accompanying you.' She nodded assent, as she had little English.

Tuesday, May 15*th,* 1798.—We had a most pleasant outing to-day, and we caught a good many fish, which we forthwith proceeded to eat for dinner, arranging ourselves on the grass. Vrow van Rhenin lighted the fire and cooked the fish, and most excellent it was. After luncheon we hauled again with nets ; they produced a huge skate as large as a house, which sighed bitterly and died with difficulty. It was ordered into oil. There were a great many little fish like eels with it ; they have bills like woodcocks, and are called Bacchus fish. We asked van Rhenin how he came to settle so far away from human habitation. He said that he had spent a long time in Cape Town, but did not like it. ' My wife said she did not mind where she lived so long as it was with me. I have therefore chosen a place where, by breeding horses, I can always make a gain ; and as I have a taste for sport, by hunting and fishing I keep my table well provided. I am perfectly contented and happy, and so is *meine vrow.* I am now independent, and away from rivalry, and I am beloved and respected. The first does not mortify, the latter does not flatter me. But we are forgetting to put to the horses.' ' That is the first bit of philosophy,' said Mr. Barnard, 'I have heard since I left Berkeley Square.' We both united in liking this man, his wife, his children, his horses, his fish, and everything to do with him.

Thursday, May 17th, 1798.—We spent yesterday at the van Rhenins—nothing more exciting than a set off after zebras. This morning we left the van Rhenins at eight, and Jacob accompanied us for a day or two. We knew not how to repay our host for all his kindness. Mr. Barnard therefore made him a present of a gun, and I gave his wife a smelling-bottle with a double gold top. We also gave the children ribbands, and among the slaves we distributed our handkerchiefs, scissors, thread, needles, etc. We drove over a pathless road among the mountains, where no trace of human creature or blade of grass was to be seen. It was very hilly and healthy pasturage ground, and we saw a good deal of game, troops of bontebocks and zebras. We reached the Landdrost's of Swellendam about seven o'clock, after again crossing the abominable Stony River. We were received in great style by the Landdrost, the prince of the place.

Monday, May 21st, 1798.—The last few days we spent quietly here waiting for our guide, without whom we could not proceed on our journey. On Sunday we attended Divine service; the audience was reverent and attentive, but in natural elegance the Hottentot congregation I told you of beat this hollow. I never beheld so large and fat a collection of human beings together before. There were eight women on the first row, who each could not weigh less than from fifteen to thirty stone, and the men were the same, though they were not in general so fat, but they were taller. Some of the young Boers, however, had fine countenances, and two or three of the women were not bad-looking, of the florid type which Rubens would have loved. There were a good many *kinder* baptized, the boys in their little men's nightcaps; they had three names apiece.

The next morning we set off, our guide having come. We went off in state, for as we started a flag was hoisted, and the sound of cannon surprised me. It was a compliment paid to the Secretary as a representative of His Gracious Majesty King George. We dined at a farmhouse, where we were received by the *vrow*—a house unworthy of such a mistress; she was larger than the mansion. After dinner I begged our guide, Mynheer Prince, who had to interpret for us, to invite the *vrow* and her husband to meet me at the Castle when they came to the Cape, and desired him once for all to ask every Boer and his wife who showed us any civility on this journey. He stared at me. 'Are you serious?' said he. 'Certainly,' said I; 'I feel obliged to them—they give me what they have, and will hardly accept payment in return.' 'Nay,' said he, 'you are perfectly right, but I never heard any English talk of returning a civility in all my life.' 'The more shame to them,' said I. He spoke to the *vrow*, and she nodded assent, which is the Dutch fashion, very few words being used on such occasions. This settled, we shook hands and left them, but not them only. Their stoep was covered with a set of large idle Boers in their blue jackets, sons of the family, men who did hardly anything beyond eating and smoking, scarcely superintending the work of the farm, which is carried on by slaves. They regarded us with great curiosity, but I saw no hostility; I believe the farmers are better contented with the English Government than the people in the town; yet all benefit by it, except a few who have lost monopolies and cannot encroach on the rights of the weak in their farms distant from Cape Town. Can there be a greater proof of the flourishing condition of this Colony, compared to what it was formerly, than the complaint of the President of the Court of Justice, who says there is not above one bankruptcy in a hundred to what there used to be?—and even the *hangman* declares he has no longer anything to do. All this is very flattering testimony in favour of English jurisdiction.

Tuesday, May 22nd, 1798.— We passed the night at the house of one Jacob Coradi. Next morning the family were all dressed and had drunk their dish of coffee before we appeared; they rise by candlelight here all the year round, stinting themselves of sleep, but they made amends for short nights by taking two hours' nap in bed after dinner every day. Mr. Barnard made his toilet in the corner, very much embarrassed by the young *vrows*, who attended him through all the manœuvrings of a tidy man's morning ablutions. They evinced much curiosity; a toothbrush they had never seen before, nor, indeed, anything else much, combs excepted. I went into the kitchen—the roof was hung as full of dried meats of many kinds as the Drup Kelder was of petrifactions, chiefly of mutton and buck.

We got into our waggon after breakfast and proceeded on our journey, falling down first into a valley rendered almost green by a variety of all the plants which our greenhouses in Europe are stocked with. After travelling about three hours I saw a little brook which wandered at a distance through some low bushes. I had just been regretting to Jane that I had not seen any of the Hottentot ladies in their natural but also ornamented state, the servants of the farmers being kept in too much drudgery to be vain. I had hardly expressed my regret when my good genius presented me Pharaoh's daughter in the very brook before me, washing her royal robes, one of the most picturesque creatures it was possible to see. From afar I saw my copper-coloured princess seated on a stone and all over ornaments, and making the waggon go on I slipped out and went across to her. She let me make a little sketch of her, none of the gentlemen being by, and in return I gave her some old silver lace which

I had in my workbag. Her transport on seeing it passed all bounds; she clasped her hands to adore it, tied it round her head, and then took it off and spread it out on the bushes. She was really a very gallant-looking girl of eighteen, and most good-natured.

We had a terrible experience this night, which we spent at the Brandt Fly Baths, an exceedingly dirty place, where the food baffled description. We could eat nothing, and I declared that, as I never ate supper, I must beg permission of the *vrow* to have my tea and bread and butter; I only wanted some boiling water, as I had all the rest by me. Jane, however, would not join us, but retired to bed in silent despair. I found her later laid out for the night in her powdering gown. We spent an awful night, all bitten to death with fleas.

Wednesday, May 23rd, 1798.—We could get no water to wash with in the house, so we went out to the spring and bathed as nature meant us to do. A most unwholesome breakfast, and then, thank goodness, we bolted off, rejoiced to be out of this abode of nastiness and vermin. We proceeded through a valley, and as we went more bold and picturesque became the mountains, some with spurs like a cathedral; trees were wanting, but the 'bones of the country' were charming. We dined at a most comfortable farm-house, and so clean and tidy was it that we determined to stay here for the night, and retired to roost betimes.

Thursday, May 24th, 1798.—We were scarcely out of bed when all the *vrows* and slaves invaded our rooms. I saw from the anxious eyes which darted into my boxes that, though they liked to give, they also wished to receive; so I gave the young ones all the ribbands and beads I could spare, tea and sugar to the mothers, and handkerchiefs to the slaves. This day we proceeded to the Roysand Kloof, a very long pass, up which we were obliged to walk, the waggon slowly dragging on before, the road very bad but romantic. As we reached the summit the sun was beginning to set, with a glow of orange ray, to the left behind the hills, and made a magnificent spectacle. Soon after it began to get dark. By the time we reached the house of Mynheer Duval, a wealthy man of rather higher class than the other Boers, the darkness had overwhelmed us.

Saturday, May 26th, 1798.—We spent yesterday at the Duvals', where nothing of importance occurred, and nothing much of interest, for everybody was wealthy and flourishing. This morning we left them, and travelled far on a very bad road. At last it became deep sand up to the axletrees. We reached Mynheer Slaber's, where we slept, and we spent the next day (Sunday) there, and also Monday and Tuesday, making excursions in the neighbourhood.

Wednesday, May 30th, 1798.—We started off, on the return journey now, departing at ten o'clock. The gentlemen mounted their horses to shoot on the way to Groene Kloof, where we proposed to dine and stay all night. It is a Government post, where dragoons are quartered, a most excellent house, stabling, offices, and farm, but we found all much out of repair. There was a fine view of the Cape from the rising ground at the back of the house.

Thursday, May 31*st*, 1798.—This was the last day of our tour. We remounted our waggon at ten, and started off for a farmhouse called Blueburg, where we dined; roads much the same as usual, healthy sand, scarce in cultivation or grass. After dinner, Gaspar, to save some heavy road, drove down upon the sea-beach before we came to the Salt River, a piece sometimes dangerous from quicksands. Unfortunately he had mistaken the hour, and imagined the tide was retreating, instead of which it was coming in. Every five minutes he was obliged to whip up his horses to their full speed to avoid sinking into sands almost alive from the sea which foamed under our wheels. We were very much afraid, and that not without reason. However, the fact justified Gaspar, for we got through all safe, and by eight o'clock at night, accompanied by a heavy south-easter, arrived at the Castle and home.

IX

The Castle, Cape of Good Hope:
August 13th, 1798.

'A SOFT word,' saith the Proverbs, 'turneth aside wrath.' And the repetition of a kind expression from the mouth of a friend who, I began to fear, was forgetting me entirely, is so conciliatory, and so satisfactory, that it is impossible to do anything else than to fly to pen and ink to hold a little mental communication. Why—why do you express yourself kindly of me and of my husband, and say you have pleasure in my letters, and even honour me so unexpectedly far as to quote information from them, yet never tell me so yourself by one line? Remember that (in spite of Doctor De Maineduc's doctrines) one cannot be quite sure at the far end of the globe, without the intervention of a little pen and ink, what one's well-beloved *antipode* is feeling for one. But you have, to more than one, said obliging things of me, for which I thank you, less because they were flattering than because they sweep away a set of little, vile, painful suggestions which began to haunt me, and which have rendered me silent for the last three or four weeks when I had plenty to say to you, and when 'old love and kindness' would have been glad, if pride had not laid its heavy embargo on all scribbling till you should say 'Go on and prosper, and tell me all, without fancying yourself tiresome or being ashamed.' All you shall have, and that directly—for there is a signal for three ships from the north-west; and, if any more arrive from England without my hearing from you, I will not answer that I mayn't relapse, and then I shall not be able to get over the ground with any comfort to you or myself. At present I have a fair field for hope; and even if I should be disappointed, the letters of my two good-natured friends about you, and a message or two from yourself through Lord Macartney, will last me a little while longer.

We remained for some weeks at Paradise after our return from our tour into the interior, rising with the sun and inhaling the fresh morning air at the back of the Table Mountain. The greatest fault of this situation is, that we have about two hours less of his Majesty Sol than if we were on the other side of the hill, as he is set to us when he shines on the rest of the world. The only experience this short residence in the country gave us was, that whoever means to build anything in Africa (Mr. Barnard was building a kitchen) must do it in the height of summer, when the heat may dry the clay and lime quickly. It approached the rainy season when ours was roofing in with rushes. The consequence was, that a heavy shower swelled the raw mortar and 'down dropped Dido,' which involved the loss of the conveniency it would have been, and the discomfiture of Mr. Barnard's project and the expense of the materials. As to the labour, the walls had been run up by a couple of dragoons from a military quarter at the bottom of the mountain— and a very great advantage it is to have a few days of one or two of his Majesty's scarlet coats occasionally, in a country where artificers are not to be had, or, if obtained with difficulty, are to be paid with still greater difficulty. A soldier to whom we give 1s. 6d. per day, his fare, and wine will do more in one day than a Dutchman or slave in three, for a dollar a day.

The largest chestnuts I ever saw by many, many degrees were here. I collected a bag for you, but on cracking one, two months after, I found it quite withered and gone, unworthy therefore to be sent. I must plant a few to convey them safe. At Paradise I had hoped to have had all sorts of good things—poultry, pigs, garden stuff, and fruit—but the first I could not keep, as they wandered and were lost amongst the heaths, sugar trees, and silver trees with which the hill is covered half-way up. Pigs had the same reason against them; they would have certainly preferred a state of freedom and acorns to my chains. Garden stuff can hardly be raised—the soil is so cold on that side of the mountain, and, except pears, the fruit trees are all gone. Troops of monkeys from the hills considerably annoyed the gardener. He shot, and shot, but no lives were lost, and as the pears are of a kind to ripen and decay all at once, I mean this year to stipulate that the monkeys may have their fill—they are the old proprietors. We cut two or three beautiful walks on a sort of terrace which looks to the sea and the Hottentot mountains; the bushes on each side gave it shade. I must make a sketch of this, and the noble rock as it rises above, for you; but how many things I propose to do!—how few execute from want of time!

I was sorry that we saw so little of Lord Hobart [1] in consequence of our tour into the interior. He is a pleasant man, but seemed to me to feel rather mortified at having his face turned to England instead of Bengal. I could not get him to enter on the subject of Lord Mornington at all, which corroborated this. On the contrary, Lord Mornington was constantly talking of Lord Hobart, and presupposing the pleasure of their meeting. As to the Anstruthers,[2] I have loved him as a good friend all my life, but she is a sad fool. If there could be two opinions about this, I would not say so to *you*, but she always has been reckoned ill-tempered, and this

---

[1] Robert Hobart, Lord Hobart (later fourth Earl of Buckinghamshire) had been Governor of Madras, and was returning to England. He stopped at the Cape on his way home to meet Lord Mornington. He was disappointed at not being made Governor-General of India, as he had been given to expect.

[2] Sir John and Lady Anstruther.

new greatness which you have bestowed on her, through Sir John,[1] has turned her poor head quite round. She would not allow Lord Mornington to know anything. 'Sir *Jann*,' as she called him, was the fountain-head of all political intelligence, and after she had disgusted him with her foolish vanity, she bewailed to Lord Hobart later on (whom she very much courted) that he was not to be Governor-General instead of the other. What a blessing to Lord Mornington, who is a domestic man and fond of women's company, if he had had the pleasant, judicious, good Lady Strange for his first lady in command instead of this Begum, who goes with powerful intentions of changing all old customs that are disagreeable to her. 'And if she tries to change one of them,' says General Baird, 'she will live alone.'

We were scarce returned from our month's absence up the country when the Stranges and the Clives arrived. We certainly should have asked Lord and Lady Clive[2] to take part of our 'pot luck' at the Castle as old friends, which both were—she of mine, Lord Clive of Mr. Barnard at Naples. But the near connection with Lady Strange, she being also Lady Hardwicke's particular friend, and their having less money to spare for Cape expenses, which are not light, determined us to invite them and their ward, Miss Roberts, to reside with us, rather than

---

[1] Sir John was made Chief Justice of Bengal.
[2] Lord Clive was the new Governor of Bengal.

ask the greater personages. The Stranges did so during their stay here, which was two or three weeks. He bears a high character amongst all who know him, and I am convinced a deserved one. She is a happy creature at getting away from the East Nook of Fife to be the Lady Recorder at Madras. She and Lady Clive will get on like lambs. What a sensible, pleasant, and happy woman Lady Clive is! She has a mind open to receive pleasure from everything, to please as far as she can, is incapable of offending, and will not tire, I am sure, of any situation she is placed in. But how comes it that they are going at all? People so wealthy—a man apparently so little ambitious! By implication, though not by direct words, I had reason to think the matter was offered to him, and I did not think Administration—any Administration I mean—was so rich in great appointments as to give without the boon being solicited. Perhaps his *name* is held to be a lucky one to go to India. He seems in good spirits, but says little, and when he visits, wise man, has Mr. Petrie always with him. To me he used to come alone, and we talked of everything *but* Madras or Governments. To them succeeded Lord and Lady Teignmouth, who have reached you ere now. Never saw I such a succession of Governors—the sea has been quite covered with them for the last six months.

Happy shall I be if it sees nothing of the departure of our *own* dear Governor, Lord Macartney, for some time yet. I have ever thought he would stay till the beginning of the year 1799, and I believe I shall be proved a witch. I wish I could give him a right fit of the gout and lodge it in his toe—it jumps about his stomach and head, and sometimes a little affects his spirits, but never the force and firmness of his mind, which, when called upon, can rally and rise above pain. It is wonderful to hear how he can jest and talk away with memory and fancy at a time when (his company gone) he can hardly support himself.

By the way, I know not how it comes into my head *now*, what is an old story by this time—a very silly and ill-natured account of the races here, written and sent home by some dull wits with whom the Cape was a good deal infested at one time. There certainly *were* races here, but Lord Macartney, whose servant is stated to have broken his leg in riding one, not only had no horse, but privately disapproved of there being races at all, and did not subscribe. Mr. Barnard did the same. He declined being a member of what they call the 'Turf Club,' and out of a little pique they call him in the papers the 'life and soul of the turf.' This was untrue, for he went into the country to avoid them. I gave my ten pagodas to the ladies' purse, as two other ladies of my own rank in society had subscribed their names to it without consulting me, and I did not like to throw a tacit stricture on them by refusing mine, or run the risk of being called shabby, though privately I liked no part of the business, thinking the Colony too much in its infancy for a sort of amusement which would be likely to introduce with it many other foolish things. But where there is a great body of idle young men, with a few ladies not ill-disposed to co-operate in any plan of amusement, one cannot be too cautious of appearing to set up as a reformer, if one wishes, as I do, to possess universal goodwill. With respect to the faro tables, to my great sorrow I found that the great good-nature of Colonel Hope (who is, sure, one of the best-conditioned good creatures in the world) had been over-persuaded by a Mr. Bird, Deputy-Quartermaster under General Fraser, a young man who seems to love play, to hold a bank with him during these races. Mr. Barnard, I have reason to think, hinted this privately to the Governor, who sent a message to desire it might be the first and last time he heard of such a thing in this Colony. In Lord Macartney's house there are no cards, and at my assemblies and balls only half-crown whist or casino, but no game of chance is allowed. If people don't like the rules of our house they will not come to it. As to the 'ostentatious splendour' of my appearance on the race-ground, though possessed of the neatest chariot and four in the Colony, the only day I appeared there I was in the carriage of a Dutchman, with his wife and family, not in my own—very much quizzed indeed by my countrymen and women for being with the Dutch, but very well pleased to give this public testimony that the Secretary's wife wished to connect herself as much with the people of the country as they chose. In the course of the morning how angry I was often made by the folly and bad-breeding of the thoughtless John Bulls who were constantly galloping up to the carriage I was in, obviously a Dutch one, to bid me remark the figures that were to run the Dutch race. 'Lord, what a saddle!' 'Ye Gods, what a bridle!' 'I would give twenty guineas to see that one thrown—ay, and his neck broke!' 'How he would kick in his demi-pique!' etc. etc.—holding all the Dutch in such contempt, and forgetting that the company I was with were not *all* deaf, and some of them might understand English enough to comprehend an insult. I believe I remarked in a former letter that it is the supercilious mode in which the Dutch find themselves treated by the English here which makes them partly prefer French insincerity and French *politesse*. But to return. Lord Macartney is as much displeased with this same newspaper wit as a great man can be with a little matter; and I, a little great woman, am displeased enough with it to make it a great matter by having thus taken up your time with the exposition of the truth.

September 22nd.—So far had I got, my dear friend, when I was seized with a sore-throat which confined me for a fortnight to bed, and a week more in my own room. Nothing did me any good till a charming packet of letters arrived from England, and one from you amongst the rest. '*My dear Lady Anne*' at the top, in your great colossal hand delighted my eyes, but the hand of another succeeded to it.

Alas! it was not Lady Jane's, as I thought, and I am sadly afraid that your eyes must have been very weak to have forced you to employ an amanuensis. You say many very kind, very flattering things to me, *too* flattering, was it not that I know where you feel kindness you are a most partial judge. You cannot be too much so to please me; may I never be judged impartially of by those I love. Nothing alloyed the pleasure these very agreeable compliments gave me except their being written in another man's hand; but as I found '*Adieu, my dear friend*' in your own, with '*Henry Dundas*' to the bottom in pledge of your sincerity, I was perfectly contented, and now I shall go on as before, scribbling away from such funds as this place gives me, without a fear of your being tired or annoyed.

Was it not that here is Mr. Maxwell come to tell me that he must have my letters in ten minutes, as the Government box is to be sealed up, I would give you a couple of pages of Gazette—I mean a set of such Cape anecdotes as have taken place since I wrote to you last, some of them curious enough—but I will reserve that for my next letter; it is possible I may have still two or three days more to write in.

September 24th.—This is very charming—I find I am likely to have still another day or two before the little, hasty vessel is permitted to sail which carries this to St. Helena. The Government box is made up, I believe, and why the ship does not sail immediately I know not; but I am glad of it, as it gives me a few hours to add another letter to the stupid one already put up for you, which contains little, except growling at yourself, and forgiving.

This shall be the Gazette I promised of all the Cape occurrences since I last wrote to you. Small as the place is, there is a wonderful number of little *bizarre* incidents, half-European, half-African, which make as good gossip for those who like it as if the actors were dukes and ladyships. What happens to be talked of before me I hear, because I have a pair of ears, but no one brings me a secret or a wonder, because it is known that I am not fond of tittle-tattle. At the same time, observe that I am going to write a perfect tittle-tattle letter to you in the midst of all my discretion and rigidity. 'Tis the way with all prudes to frown publicly at what they privately smile. I shall not confine myself, however, to anything, but bring out everything as it comes into my mind, having no time for arrangement. We have had elopements, marriages, half-marriages, marriages to be. We have been taking prizes, had ships in distress, and Beauties that went to Bengal last year to be married, married and returning for their health. The oddest occurrence that presents itself is the wedding of a mad Captain Barclay, who insisted on having a licence to marry a woman whose character was so *very* bad that Lord Macartney sent Mr. Barnard to advise him against it. Tell your Lord,' said he, ' that I am forty-five years of age, and should know what I like.' As that would not do, Mr. Barnard next hinted that report actually circulated it that he (Captain Barclay) was married already, and of course a licence could not be given. This he denied, and professed himself ready to take his oath before the Fiscal that he was single. He did so, and was married next day. He now says that he is perfectly certain he is justified in taking that oath, as his wife by the last letters was so ill that he is *sure* she must be dead by now! The present one will suffer no loss if he separates from her, as it is supposed he will do soon. He has a brother, a man of honour and credit, in England. I fear he will get a poor account of some bills he sent for the purchasing him out of the regiment.

Soon after this a fair lady eloped with the purser of an Indiaman. Mr. Barnard was also sent to prevail on her to return to her colours, but she would not, and is with the purser still. We had next the elopement of the Dutch Miss Vandenberg with Captain Hamilton Ross, a young man of very good character, who had made fair and honourable proposals which the father objected to, having a right to keep her fortune till she was eighteen if she married without his consent. Meantime his own wife died, and he informed his daughter that he meant to give her for a mother-in-law a person who had been in the habit of whipping her, and who had a son who was intended for her husband. She told him if he did that she would marry Captain Ross. The father married.

The young lady chucked the Dutch lover under the chin for a few days to lull suspicion, and then went off. The father has been roaring like a madman to catch her, but she is where no one can get at her. His rage is so loud that it has even reached the tars on board of their ships. One of the Jacks lately came to him and told him, if he would swear to keep the secret and give him the reward of 100 dollars, he would show him the house where the Beauty was secreted. The father agreed, and paid him the money, forgetting his caution in his eagerness for revenge. John Bull led him in the dark through street after street; at last, breaking suddenly from him, he bid him good-night and, turning down a by-corner, was out of sight in a moment. Captain Hamilton Ross is an officer in the Scots Brigade, and his fair lady sails with him to India, and will be married there when she is eighteen, but she has a year to wait. It makes no difference; her lover is a man of perfect integrity, and she may depend on him. He has offered so fair, and behaved so well as to conciliate everybody's esteem, and whenever she is married the English ladies of the Cape, and I for one, will support her through. Her father only is to blame, and avarice is at the bottom. The Dutch ladies will not visit her, I dare say. She has a dash of the *bleu*, her mother's mother having been a slave, and as we are as proud as Lucifer on point of birth, there is no quality or virtue, not even the virtue of being rich, which is not sponged out by the word ' slave-born,' or half-caste. She is a very pretty girl—much genteeler than the generality of the women here; but I have much offended two of the Quality by asking if they were acquainted with her.

There is a Miss Du Wat who sails for England with the first ships, after a Captain Manning. He proposed to her, but she could not make up her mind about leaving her friends, and, what was of still more consequence, she could not make up her wedding clothes in time to sail on a certain day. I should not have thought *that* was of much importance, but I have heard they esteem it so here. Well, the lover embarked, and the lady began to repent that she had not accompanied him. She now means to follow him to England, against the advice of all the Englishmen here, who think she had better remain where she is. It is a bold undertaking, and justifies the old proverb, 'A stitch in time saves nine.' A stitch in her wedding clothes, more hastily put in, would have certainly saved her a most precarious sailing match.

Within these two days another fair one has eloped with another officer. She, too, being under age, is taken up by the Fiscal and in prison, but as the lover says she never proposed, or even hinted, marriage to him, I suppose this will blow by without any Hymen in the case. The Cape young ladies seem to have no dislike for our English officers, but I think they risk a little too much to secure them. They are not all like Captain Ross.

A Dutch wedding that took place lately entertained me a good deal. The master of the family has been supposed rather of the Jacobin sort,[1] and Lord Macartney was not a little displeased to find he had sent out his invitations to his friends for the wedding and ball to 'Citizen' *this* and 'Citizen' *that*—a title not permitted in this Colony, of course. No notice was taken of this till

> They were in the midst of all their din—Tra-fa-limoni-didle.
> In came the Cat, and her Kit-tin—Lam-mend and ledilly.

The cat appeared in the shape of the Town Mayor and the Kitten as twenty dragoons, who arrived in time for the ball, and put the party into a glorious fright. Mynheer instantly began stroking down the whiskers of the Town Mayor, and noble ones has that pussie, frizzled out on each side of his face. He was invited to dance, and the whole thing was treated as a jest. Mynheer professed himself ready to make the Governor every apology he could desire for his foolish method of naming his friends, which he declared to be a *jeu d'esprit only*. The Town Mayor was beginning to dance with the daughter of the family, when he saw standing above him General Dundas's cook just ready to lead off, which made him retire in disgust. The cook had asked the General's

---

[1] Lord Macartney was very anti-Jacobin, and very sternly repressed any exhibition of republican principles. This particular man was Hendrik Eckstein, and he was required at once 'to retract and redress in the most public manner this wanton and petulant conduct, or to repair to that country where, in the midst of confusion and medley, his meditations would be better relished.' Eckstein retracted.

leave in the morning to go to a neighbour *pour faire des patties*. He is a Frenchman—and all other things which that class of Frenchman are. He did not tell the General that he was *pour faire doux yeux aussi*.

We are glad to have the Navy back again in the Bay. The Bluecoats make the place cheerful. I like Sir Hugh Christian much, as an agreeable man in society. I liked the last Admiral too—Pringle; he was a growler with his tongue, as I have often told you, but I believe as honest and liberal a man in his conduct as possible. With many opportunities here of tempting his fortune, I fancy no conduct could be purer. I say the more on this, poor fellow, as I dare say he is not on good terms with anybody at home, because he cannot be prudent with that unruly little member of his, the tongue. I think Sir Hugh has rather better hopes of the nautical possibility of navigating round the coast than Admiral Pringle or others before him have had. Whether this is founded on sound sense, or the pride of superior genius, time will show. One thing I can see, who am no witch, that as vessels this year have been cruising about, at a season and round points which they formerly durst not have looked at, there is certainly less fear now of the shore round us than there was, or danger has become more familiar.

A ship was lately driven in distress to a bay—I think they call it Algoa Bay—where some of the passengers left it and came by land. The captain and others have dined often with us, and the gentlemen who came by land arrived, and dined with us, yesterday. They describe the country (as it has also appeared to us in our time) as bare, but the soil good and people hospitable and hearty. There is another ship, the 'Ganges,' which contains some English captains on their way home—one of the name of Lambert, another Broughton, the last a thin little fellow whom I believe you sent on a voyage of discovery. His vessel has been lost. He mentions an island near Japan, where he was kindly treated by a gentle race of people entirely covered with hair, and their manners mild and humane[1]—no tails—so I fancy they will class in finely at a point in Hunter's gradations, from Mr. Pitt down to the least little monkey of the forest—there being a link or two wanting, I have heard say, between negro and ourang-outang which this sweet island will afford a means of supplying.

I wonder if the races here, now going forwards, will produce any more lying paragraphs. Remember, I take the earliest opportunity to tell you *not* to believe any about me, as I have not been there at all, nor Lord Macartney nor Mr. Barnard. My former letter has told you all about that matter; but when people don't stick to truth, perhaps I shall be put in as drawn by elephants this time. I must write a letter to my cousin, Lady Dalrymple—she will be frightened when she sees that her son Johnnie has won a purse; and yet it happened so naturally that

[1] The hairy Ainu.

there was no harm in it. A great many East India gentlemen being here, they liberally proposed making a purse, and I believe all horses of all sorts were permitted to run. Johnnie's horse was a tolerable one, with some bottom. A friend offered to ride it for him, which he did; seventeen horses started for fifty guineas, and Johnnie, to his astonishment, won the purse, and is, I believe, the happiest creature now in Africa. But I must not have his mother suppose him a jockey for that. He has volunteered to go on with his regiment to India, and then returns home.

Our bay is full of ships at present, and Cape Town, I am told by a skilful merchant here, is stocked with European goods enough to last for three years, but all are locked up out of sight, and the prices remain as high as ever. In spite of this we make our ends meet—and to say the truth they encompass a good deal; but it all goes in giving good fare to others—no drinking or parade, God knows, but the solid enjoyment of making others as happy as we can.

Mr. Barnard is greatly flattered by your kindness, for he thinks he derives from you the increase of his salary by 500$l.$ a year. Though the money is convenient, the testimony of your and Lord Macartney's being pleased with him goes nearer his heart. Sorry we are that Lord Macartney talks of leaving us in two or three months, but perhaps he may still lengthen it out a little more. Mr. Barnard has fully determined to do anything that possibility can put in his power to give satisfaction to General Dundas,[1] and friendly as well as official assistance. But I tell you, in the perfect confidence of friendship, that he is a little afraid, from the General's manner, that he is not disposed to like him. It is, I am convinced, *but* manner. How can it be otherwise where unremitting attention is paid? The General is hasty, and he has not learnt that charming page in Lord Macartney's book, to respect and mark respect to others in their departments, in order to have it from them; but hurriedly and hastily does as he feels at the moment, and, I suppose, privately repents at leisure. But Mr. Barnard, though a high-minded man, is so uncommonly mild in temper that I have no fears, as I believe what he suspects is mere manner, and have not a doubt that they will get on perfectly well, with caution on the one part to counteract any little impetuosity on the other. Is not this talking with the relying confidence of friendship, when I am venturing to speak of your nephew and my husband? But you know the one party, and will not think it unnatural for me to have let my private thoughts escape to you on a subject so intimately connected with all that is interesting to me. Mr. Barnard would not be pleased with me if he knew I had said thus much, therefore I shall not tell him I have. But I do not think I am wrong.

[1] General Francis Dundas was to be appointed Acting-Governor in the absence of Lord Macartney.

On looking over the former sheet I see I have expressed myself about this new island near Japan as if it was a jest, but it is not so, and I fancy will be found rather a curious matter. I asked the Captain to show me the drawings he had had taken of the people and their costume, but I perceived from the distress of his countenance that he wished to evade letting anyone see them, and have since heard he means, with the approbation of his superiors, to publish the account with plates.

We have had most wonderful bad weather this winter; four months have elapsed, or nearly that, with very few days escaping without rain—sometimes it falls in deluges. The winds have been also extremely high, hailstones of considerable size, lightning and thunder three or four times, and on the seas I believe very severe tempests. Last winter, one week excepted, was as mild as this has been the contrary. I am really tired of the rain and of the cold, which has forced us to have fires very often, in spite of our having, what is very uncommon here, our rooms well carpeted over. By the bye, I have not mentioned yet in my Gazette what you no doubt already know—that we have found coal here. I fancy it is not of a very good quality, else I should see people more elated about it. We have tried it, but it lights with difficulty, and we have generally mixed it with English coals, some chaldrons of which we got out before the coal was found. They stood us between nine and ten pounds a chaldron at the Castle; but at that price whatever we could spare was gladly taken from us. However, whether good or bad, *any* coal, or anything to burn, so near the Cape as fifteen miles is a great *pis aller*, as wood must become more and more scarce, the more inhabited the Cape is, all being cut down for fuel, and no one replacing a bush with an acorn. We have some hopes that we have also found the coarse silkworm which makes the Bengal common silk. Doctor Roxburgh apprehends it is the same, but mynheer will not be at the pains to cultivate it. That will fall to the lot of some industrious Englishman, if you keep the Cape. We have also found water at Hutches' Bay, which will be a good thing if the quantity is sufficient; it is said it is, but I do not believe it.

Are you tired of me yet? I think I see you shake your head, and say, 'Upon my word I have some reason.' Indeed you have, but always look at meanings and motives to find apology for frivolity, dulness, or prolixity. I'll add no more, except kindest love to your ladies, and to renew my promise of writing to Lady Jane by the next ship. There is a little something I want her to do for me, but I know not whether it will be worthy of passing through her hands. God bless you, my dear friend; keep your health well for the sake of all at home and all abroad.

X

The Castle, Cape of Good Hope :
November 10th, 1798.

SORRY am I, my dear Friend, at the departure of our own dear Governor, who this day leaves the Garden House and takes up his residence with us during the short time which will be necessary to get all arranged for his leaving the Colony. If he felt he could have stayed longer with safety to himself I am convinced he would ; but the gout hangs constantly over him, never fixing itself properly, and often making him feel himself hardly more than the tenant of the hour. I wish that I had not to add that the poor Admiral, Sir Hugh Christian, seems to be still worse than Lord Macartney ; he has never enjoyed his health since his arrival, and lately, when at Saldane Bay, had an attack so violent as to lie for dead for a short time. I have my fears that he will not find it possible to remain here long ; and I shall be sorry for it, as I take him to be an excellent officer, and zealously eager to fill his part in his profession to his own honour and the good of his country. But his mind is too ardent and anxious for the strength of his poor constitution.

I have put up a specimen to you and to Mr. Pitt of what my friends the Hottentots do. I believe I mentioned this in my last letter. A couple of knives made at the Moravian Settlement, and a couple of walking-sticks made of wood, I own, with some little notion of drawing. I believe they will be the first that ever crossed the Line. Pray present these humble offerings to Mr. Pitt, with the *vrow* Barnard's very best wishes that God Almighty may long continue him and you to take care of us at home and abroad.

I will not trouble you by adding more at present. You have greater things to mind, and I have to-day to make some preparations for a bunch of wedding people in the evening, whom I have invited to introduce to our Governor before his departure. Our officers have of late been marrying the Dutch *vrows* at a great rate, and it is right to show them every civility possible, when so married, without minding their pedigree, which is sometimes not very correct. The evening is the time when they like best to visit me. Not so the Boers from the country, who generally come to pay their respects at the Castle at seven o'clock in the morning, and always have their *topi* of gin with me while I am at breakfast. I am glad to see the country people, who were civil to us when amongst them, coming to see us in return here; it marks a confidence in the assurances I made them of their being welcome. In the Dutch time none of the Boers durst presume to enter the gates of the Castle with their hats on. Now they come in freely, and some of the *vrows* bestow their kisses both on me and my better half very liberally; however, their heartiness pleases and flatters us. But I am running on. God bless you.

XI

Paradise, Cape of Good Hope:
April 4th, 1799.

FIRST, my dear Friend, let me in three cheers express my joy on the late glorious event, which I daresay will form as bright a moment in history as England ever saw.[1] Light gains double by shadow, and dark indeed was the shadow which preluded these victories. I see the new peer is to be Lord Nile, or Lord Something of the Nile. (I hope his eldest son won't be Baron Crocodile.) I should like to see a dozen more such creations.[2]

I find a considerable difference in the climate this last season, to what it was the first I arrived. This summer has been much warmer, the south-easters more violent, and the weather more various. In spite of that, I still think the climate a very pleasant one, and prodigious as the vicissitudes of heat, hot, calm, and storm in one day are, it is surprising to observe how few colds are caught. One singular effect of atmosphere I observe in

---

[1] The Battle of the Nile.
[2] Nelson was created Baron Nelson of the Nile and of Burnham Thorpe in Norfolk.

myself. When in the Castle, close by the sea shore, at Cape Town, I am constantly hoarse and cannot sing a note, but when at Paradise, which is reckoned the dampest situation, and the most dangerous for that reason in the Colony, my voice is as clear as it was when I was sixteen. I do not look quite so *young*; however, there is no help for that—'One cannot eat one's cake and have it too.' If my friends will pardon a few wrinkles on my face, I will pardon as many as they please on theirs, and reckon them only reasons for loving them the more, as it proves I have known them long.

While all goes fair and well with you in England we have got our little bit of insurrection here, at a distant part of the country, Graaf Reinet. The old bad news, I suppose (and none of the modern good yet), has travelled there, and inspired the Boers with the desire of kicking up a dust, and trying if they can't be masters still. It is nonsense for me to pretend to give you any account of matters, which the General, of course, must convey to you at length. Yet there is a possibility that this ship may sail without his dispatches, as I hear he is at Stellenbosch. So I will say what I can. These Graaf-Reinet Boers have always been turbulent and unwilling to bend to any laws, or to the Landdrost.[1] They particularly dislike their Landdrost, a very

[1] They had made an attempt to escape from the rule of the Dutch East India Company, and under its *régime* were in a state of chronic rebellion.

good sort of man, I hear, and affect to think themselves ill-used, now that they are British subjects, in not having an English Landdrost. But I believe this is a mere pretext to get rid of the present one. The ground of the present quarrel is their having forced him (and the soldiers who had the charge of a prisoner[1]) to give up to them the said prisoner, who is one of the most seditious amongst them, and was for wrong practices of some kind sent to the Cape by the Landdrost. They threatened the Landdrost's life, and from that time have kept him in constant fear by a sort of guard being placed on him that he may not run away. General Dundas sent General Vandeleur there with a party of horse, also Major Abercrombie, and one or two small vessels with troops. It was the general idea that the seditious people would instantly be reduced to order by the sight of the scarlet coats, and would surrender their arms, but I hear that they have retreated, it is thought into the Kaffir country; and more men have been requested by General Vandeleur. I cannot say, however, that I feel at all alarmed at this; it will cost a few lives, and that is a pity, but I fancy some examples must be made to preserve peace in the Colony. One of the party having remained behind, and being desirous of joining the others by a short cut, almost lost his life, being pursued by a

[1] This prisoner was an old commandant, Adrian van Jaarsveld, who was arrested on a charge of forgery, and of setting a summons of the High Court of Justice at the Cape at defiance.

troop of buffaloes, who fairly hunted him like a hare, and the speed of his horse only saved him.

What a blessing, now that our white troops are called away to the above purpose, and others sent on to India, that the people of the Cape have that spirited old corps, the Cape Association, to trust to! A corps almost two months old, and commanded by Colonel Barnard, who of course is commanded by Lady Anne, that old and experienced officer! Her Ladyship, I hear, is soon to present the regiment with their colours, in which the Whitletomb (native of this country) is happily blended and united with the Royal Oak of Old England, a compliment her ladyship means for Mynheer (if he has *nous* to understand it). The gentlemen volunteers who compose the corps had in the original plan professed themselves in readiness, should occasion require, to stand forward with any aid in their power, but General Dundas, very naturally thinking that *that* aid could not be properly administered, unless they were drilled into the knowledge of what was to be done on emergency, mentioned the Associations in England, and their conduct, as the model for this, which hint was of course adopted. The officers were chosen by ballot, and Mr. Barnard chosen Colonel, and as he is an old soldier, the business went on so much better. All were eager in the cause, a very few gentlemen excepted, who, shy of being smiled at by the military, and disliking the sacrifice of time necessary to the field days, are no longer of the corps, much to Mr. Barnard's regret, as they are good men, though bad officers.[1]

May 14*th*, 1799.—I am adding to the above, my dear friend, my latest budget, for the ship did not sail after all. I am quite ashamed to write on such bad paper to you; but I am a farmer's wife in the country, and forgot to tell the farmer, who goes into town to market (namely, the business of the office) every day at nine o'clock, that mine was done. You will pardon it, however, not being a man of much *minutiæ* of ceremony, when a friend's, a woman's, letter is in the case. I go on cheerfully writing to you since you sent me my little dose of kindness and flattery mixed, which has done me a world of good, and, at this immense distance from you all, is necessary to invigorate and enliven one, who must, like the spider, spin chiefly from her own materials. By the bye (for you know it is my way to bring out things as they pass across my mind), are Cape spiders reckoned curiosities in England? Doctor Roxburgh tells me that they are; but I hate spiders of all sorts, handsome or ugly, so much that I should not thank anybody for giving me a bushel. Think, then, what I suffered lately, when, after having found in the bushes, as I supposed, a very large mausoleum of a silkworm like a goose's egg, I put it into my writing drawer, and some days after, on opening it, a whole legion of young spiders broke forth on me.

[1] This reads like a page of recent history—the Volunteer movement among the loyalists at the Cape to protect the Colony.

It was a spider's nest, and I had inoculated every room in the house at once, for off they ran to every hole they could find. I assure you it is needless in this country to propagate gentry of this unpleasant kind, for there is one breed of little animals of a dark complexion which are in summer the plague of society. The only comfort is, that the more a house is inhabited, the fewer there are of them.

Since I wrote last the disturbances at Graaf Reinet are happily terminated. All the seditious have submitted I hear, and two or three only remain untaken amongst the disturbers of peace and good order.[1] The Kaffirs have expressed the strongest disposition to be on friendly terms with us; so too have the Bushmen, who, possessed of nothing, were robbers rather from necessity than choice, and who by the presents of cattle, etc., conveyed to them by Lord Macartney from the English Government, are won to the love of peace and good fellowship by having something to lose.

I went with Mr. Barnard to Cape Town yesterday to see the chief of one of the tribes of what is called here the *right* Bushmen. What a courageous fine fellow that young man must be,

[1] This is not quite correct. A great number submitted, but seven of the most turbulent fled to Kaffirland, where they were joined by a band of deserters from the British army, and lived there for many years. Twenty were sent to Cape Town and placed in close confinement, and sentenced to punishment in varying degrees. None were put to death, and with the exception of one who was flogged and banished, and two who died in prison, they were all set at liberty by the Dutch High Commission in 1803 on the cession of the Colony to the Dutch.

who, after having gone on plundering a neighbouring nation (the Hottentots) for such a length of time, trusts himself with a band of them to come down (the first time a Bushman ever came voluntarily so far) to see the English Governor at the Cape! His brother only accompanied him. The chief, whose name was 'Philan'—I am willing to hope a contraction of *philander*—was covered with old military ornaments of different regiments, some of which we had brought with us from England, having stored ourselves from an old shop for such things with all the ornamental brass we could pick up. Different people had given him some *very* old clothes before he came to pay me a visit at the Castle, so I did not see him quite in his unadorned state of loveliness. But over these clothes he wore his own, the skin cloak and all his decorations—gorgets, belts, and pouches. His countenance was good-humoured to the greatest degree, with more character in it than the Hottentot face, which has rarely more than gentleness to boast of. His hair was perfectly different from the hair of any other human creature I have seen, as it was like fringes of fine knotted black worsted—such knotting as old ladies do for beds. In the front of his forehead he wore a little button, hanging down somewhat like a pagoda, and behind he had a *queu* (I don't think I have spelled this word aright), that is a pigtail, which hung down an inch, with two shells to it. I was quite delighted with the dress of the tail—it showed he was no democrat; but it is not exactly such as is worn by our captains in St. James's Street. As they speak no Dutch, and as the interpreter (a Hottentot) was obliged to leave them to fetch the rest, I could not get so much of their minds as of their faces. But they seemed much pleased with the English, and are to bring their *vrows* to visit me this winter. The Gonagua man took great pains to tell Mynheer Barnard what pretty girls there are in that country; theirs is the country described by Valliante, so perhaps there may have been some truth in his representation of 'Narina.' They have some ideas of marriage—the chief and his brother had two wives each, but one or two of the Hottentots who accompanied them only one apiece. We gave to all coarse handkerchiefs, knives, scissors, needles, thread, and beads. To the chief I gave a very fine button, which he instantly tied round his neck, and Mr. Barnard gave him a coat and waistcoat, which he also put on, throwing off his clothes to do so. Fortunately, Mr. Barnard at that time gave these two articles *only*, else I know not to what lengths the chief would have carried his toilette in my presence. There is something singularly delicate in the make of the Bushman—his arms are so finely turned and hands so small (one of the fingers of this one was withered off by the bite of a serpent). His wrist was as delicate as that of a lady's, yet when he bent his bow it seemed to be strong, and the wildness of his figure was striking—but their tones! Oh, how strangely savage! They have all the clucking noise of the Hottentots, each word being so divided, but accompanied by sounds, or rather groans, quite uncouth.

We gave them some brandy, which they greedily took, and, previous to their departure, some gimlets, and an old sword, and to each some tobacco and a new pipe. They were quite happy, and, bidding us farewell, made each a sort of bow with his hat or handkerchief in hand. The chief, rapid in his motions, made a low one; a table was near, and the tobacco-pipe (stuck in his hat), knocking against it, was shivered to pieces. Never, no never, did painting convey such an attitude, or the feelings of nature speak so plain. He did not gaze at it, or pick it up. He covered his face at once with his hand, desolation was in his heart, and he stood there till, ready to burst into tears, he could just turn aside to prevent them from dropping. Meantime we had sent for another pipe. The Hottentots *clucked* to him that here was another; he took his hand from his face—saw the pipe—received it—but the remedy to his sorrow was too sudden for the transition of joy to follow it—the pain of the broken pipe stuck, though the new pipe was in his hand. He then picked up the fragments and placed all once more in the hat, of which he seemed very proud, and with a deep sigh and a consoled ' *Tankee*,' went off. By the bye, I asked him if he had any objection to giving me a little of his queer hair and his *queue*—giving him a fine large shell to tie in its place, which enchanted him. He was greatly flattered by my request, and held down his head to have it cut off, which the brother seeing, came forwards with his fringed top also. I had meant this modern relic for Lady Jane, and had written her a note, but it looks so odd and uncouth that I think it would rather frighten than please her. Perhaps, as you are a bold man, and not easily scared, I may send it to you, or a little of his hair.

We have had two ships come into Simon's Bay within the last week in great distress—the one an old shattered vessel, containing, besides the crew, six hundred French prisoners—those who have been for some years in the prisons at Madras, and those who were lately seized at Pondicherry on suspicion, fully founded, of their carrying on machinations against our interests with their countrymen and with Tippoo. Of these there are some opulent and creditable men of good manners. They, in number about fifty, have the half of the Captain's cabin, the other 550 are stowed below. I suppose the ship came off in a hurry, but it appears as if the agent employed to provide for them had not done his employer justice, as they were more than half-famished, and in want of everything. Disease had begun to sweep them off, and it was daily gaining ground, so the General has permitted the sick to be put on shore, and they are now at Muizenburg. I wish there were the means here of affording some vessel to take away the half of them, but I hear there is at present not one *carriage* of that sort on this coast, all being cruising out. Thank Heaven, however, for the success of the British Navy over our enemies; we have little now to fear from invasion. The other ship contained convicts; it was in still greater distress for food, and in great want of medical aid. The ship surgeon is a humane man who exerts himself night and day to do his duty, but is so ignorant of his profession that he did not know there was a putrid fever on board, though eight and ten died of it a day. I have no more news, so good-bye.

XII

The Castle, Cape of Good Hope:
September 12th, 1799.

I AM told, my dear Friend, that the embargo laid on anything sailing from our coast is to be taken off now that we are strengthened by the return of our squadron, and that a vessel for England will sail in two days. The time is short for me to write to you as I could wish; but after a pause so very long, during which time we have heard nothing from England, and sent nothing to it, I cannot permit any opportunity to escape without giving you a letter, hurried though it may be. I have had the mortification of hearing that several of mine to you have been lost and some destroyed; you have therefore missed a good deal of my chit-chat. I have, however, regretted some of them the less, as we have not for a considerable period had those peaceable and safe times which produced nothing but rose-colour in our minds or correspondence. Glad I am that before you receive any news from the Cape, to give you uneasiness (temporary uneasiness only, I hope), such a fund of triumphant joy will be laid from your brilliant Indian successes as to render our Kaffir and

Hottentot war a less important feature. The fall of Tippoo [1] and the victorious six weeks' campaign of the gallant Mornington, I fancy, has about this time set your great guns a-singing. The pleasantest music in times of public danger is the music of the Tower. We have had a *feu de joie* on the occasion, and glad we were to spend a little of our powder (wanted though they say it might have been at Graaf Reinet) to awe our fellow subjects, the Dutch here, and, what is of more importance, their slaves, into some opinion of British force by our successes.

The last very long letter you have probably received from me was followed shortly by others [2] containing accounts of more fires at different parts of Cape Town, fortunately prevented from doing material harm, which, if all accidental, at least were liable to a different interpretation. To those succeeded a new species of calamity which lasted but for a short time, but threatened us all in the Castle with a watery grave. You will not suppose me to be painting only through a woman's fears, when I tell you that we were obliged to fire guns of distress. A couple of days' rain, almost amounting to the deluge of old, began the ill. Towards night (the second day) water rose so many feet suddenly in the Castle as to fill up all the ditches, go near to drown the officers of artillery in their mess-room and all the

---

[1] Seringapatam was taken by assault after a siege, in which Tippoo was killed, April 4, 1799.

[2] These letters are missing.

bandits in the lower courtyard, four of which only did suffer; but as it rose a foot or two every minute, the increasing danger appeared considerable, and while we paused the moment for flight was over. The uncertainty of the cause of this doubled the alarm. By some the sea was supposed to have broken in, others imagined it to be like the earthquake at Lisbon which was so fatal to thousands. This phenomenon, however, proved only to have been some waterspouts, or clouds loaded with rain, which broke over the Table Mountain, falling down the gullies there, where, joined by other waters from the adjacent hills, they had become a torrent impetuous enough to break down all before it, but not such as to have been dangerous had it not taken the direction of the Castle, the outer gate of which it entered in a volume of ten or twelve feet high, and the natural consequences followed from the general dismay in the dark.

Having had fire, water, and already somewhat of an insurrection in the Graaf-Reinet district, we needed only mutiny in the Army to render the measure of our vexations complete. This we had a taste of the 6th day of last month, when a plot was revealed by a soldier of the 91st Regiment, who had been solicited to join it by one M'Gie, a soldier of the 61st, who had told the other that the 81st and 61st regiments were ready at a minute's warning to assist each other to murder, or otherwise secure, their commanding officers, who slept in the

Castle; to seize the powder-magazine, take possession of the Castle, and become the new masters of the Cape. The rogue M'Gie, who was at the head of this scheme, finding it defeated by discovery, turned King's evidence under promise of pardon from the General, and, by accusing a couple of innocent men, whose excellent characters bore them through, screened his real associates, and it remains still in the dark who they were. But though there proved to be much less in the matter than was at first imagined, there still was, in the opinion of many, something; and this is an unpleasant idea to their very worthy Commanders Carruthers and Barlow, who are excellent officers and good men. They wish to think this the mad scheme of one foolish boy. It, however, put the whole garrison in alarm and reared the gallows for instant execution. None were condemned, however, for the above reasons.

This circumstance took place the day before General Dundas left Cape Town to co-operate with and effect a junction with General Vandeleur against the Kaffirs and Hottentots.[1] So far I have narrated common events on which everyone is entitled to think. It becomes a more delicate and difficult task to add our subsequent history, as in the course of it I fear I may be led to place myself in a presumptuous and improper point of view to my dear

---

[1] This was what is known in South African history as the Third Kaffir War.

friend, by throwing out opinions on the wisdom of some things going forwards in the Colony, which I have no business to touch on. Yet I love you too well to be cautious, and I know the Cape to be so favourite a child of yours that, if I, as a bystander, imagine that whipping is a worse measure than coaxing it, I think I should fail in my duty to you if I did not privately say so. Probably you will not have many letters at present. Where there is little good to be told, people are more shy of writing to a Minister than on prosperous occasions; but it is the very time when a friend's narrative, however poorly stated, may chance to be of some little use.

I mentioned in one of my last letters that General Vandeleur still remained in the northern district, after having reduced the Boers at Graaf Reinet to obedience—a measure easy to be effected from the known dastardly spirit of the Dutch here, who run from a musket or a scarlet coat; and I fancy these Boers were refractory from imagining themselves at too great a distance from the Cape to have any military force sent against them. I should have also mentioned that General Vandeleur sent as prisoners here about twenty persons, supposed to be the ringleaders of the turbulent Boers, who were immediately confined to the Castle till the pleasure of Government at home should be known respecting them. This produces a tedious delay to such as are innocent, comparatively speaking. I have heard it said that, if they had been tried by the laws of the Colony and by the judges here, those who deserved it would have been fairly condemned *now* that there is an English government to support the Courts of justice; otherwise, no Dutchman would venture to condemn a Dutchman. No sooner were these prisoners sent off from Graaf Reinet, and the remaining Boers reduced to submission, than General Dundas recalled the greater part of the troops. Had the military been permitted to have remained some time longer, perhaps it might have been more judicious, as they were at that time become eminently necessary to defend the property of the prisoners sent here, and of the Boers that remained, from the Kaffirs their neighbours. These Kaffirs, finding from the Hottentots in the service of the Boers (and now left by their wives and families with the care of the farms) that the usual ammunition which Government allows the Boers, as a necessary defence against wild beasts and plunderers, was at this time withheld for fear of its being applied to bad purposes, saw nothing to oppose their natural taste for rapine. The Dutchmen, the original cause of all, who had been rescued from the Landdrost's authority by the Boers, had sheltered themselves with the Kaffirs—not amongst the subjects of King Gaika, the friend of the English, but with this vagrant tribe, in number it is supposed about 3,000, who, driven from this country for misdemeanours some years ago, have established themselves amongst a range of wooded mountains, extending about two or three hundred miles, bounded by the dominions of King Gaika and by the Fish River behind, and on this side by the Dutch settlements. This boundary of the Fish River (which had been the accustomed one, I hear, for the Kaffirs in general) General Dundas thought it expedient that General Vandeleur should insist on their retreating behind, and to force them to do so General Vandeleur drove away their cattle to its banks, knowing they must follow for subsistence.[1]

How far it was well to force the old, old policy on this occasion you will best judge. It seems natural, however, to expect that the Kaffirs would resist, for had they been compelled to recross that river they must have found death from their countrymen on the other side, who are numerous. They of course refused, and hostilities began. On the other hand, the Hottentots I have mentioned, long habituated to oppression and unjustly treated on all occasions by the farmers, seeing no disposition (at least that they knew of) in the English to redress their wrongs, began to think this was a fair moment for them to redress themselves. They took possession of the arms and horses of their absent masters,

---

[1] Gaika's uncle, Ndlambe the regent, had headed a rebellion against him and, though defeated, had in February 1796 managed to escape. A great many tribes joined him. He now crossed the Fish River with his armed followers. As the Fish River was the boundary-line recently fixed by Lord Macartney, he thus invaded the Colony.

mounted themselves, and along with the other Hottentots, the servants of the remaining farmers, joined the Kaffirs, assisted them in resisting the attempts of the English, and in making depredations on the Dutch settlements, which they plundered and destroyed. This met with opposition from our small force, and in dividing it for different purposes an officer and twenty men were cut off.[1]

General Vandeleur wrote for more support. Our garrison was weak, and our squadron absent; our troops were hardly returned to Cape Town when they were sent 800 miles back again to effect the purposes I have mentioned, and at the same time to awe the rising spirit of rapine and cruelty which, once awakened in savage people, becomes soon desperate and dangerous. Field-pieces and more ammunition were also sent. The Dutch saw our danger from experience of 150 years, nor were they silent. 'My Lady,' said the old President of the Court of Justice (even to me), 'if I can judge of the Kaffirs now, by what I found them five years ago, when I was sent to negotiate on a quarrel between them and us, nothing will ever be made of them by force of arms. Hostilities rouse their natural taste for plunder; they have everything to gain, nothing

[1] After a gallant defence all were killed except four men, who managed to escape. General Vandeleur's company hardly formed before it was surprised by Kaffirs, who rushed on them with their assegais broken so that they could be used for stabbing. They were driven off with great slaughter. It was then that General Vandeleur sent to Cape Town for reinforcements.

to lose, and from their knowledge of the country they fight with every advantage against us—indeed they rather annoy than fight, lurking by two and three amongst the bushes and avoiding action by daylight. We have always found that to keep well with them is our only safety, and if a quarrel takes place to make it up quickly. If peace is wanted 1,000 dollars well laid out in copper, hatchets, gewgaws, etc., will do more in tempting their chiefs to amity than the expense to Government of 100,000*l*. laid out in men and ammunition.'

Lord Macartney was so much of the opinion also that it was dangerous to rouse the hornets' nest, that he never would allow anyone to molest the Kaffirs or even to permit traffic with them for fear of any difference. His known maxims on this head, together with the counsels and the experience of old Dutchmen, such as I have mentioned, could have afforded, were, one might have supposed, not wholly free from use. But I hear our friend General Dundas is too sanguine of success his own way, and has the unlucky pride of calling in no one's judgment in partnership with his own, which cannot be very experienced on such points; while his temper is so eager for *adieu*, that he does not give his own judgment fair play by a little consideration.

Day after day bringing worse accounts of families murdered, women carried off, and the quantity of men General Vandeleur was possessed of becoming equally inadequate for an offensive or defensive war, he being also at one time cut off from his main body, General Dundas declared he would 'go himself and finish the business one way or another.' But in what manner, I fancy he does not thoroughly know. The orders which followed his departure for more troops to be sent (300) were countermanded the day after, and this day re-ordered, another field-piece and 130 men being this morning sent. Mr. Barnard most anxiously ventured to recommend him to take with him some respectable persons understanding the languages of the country, and likely to be clever at negotiation, but the General said Abercrombie and M'Nab were sufficient; I hope he will find them so. I have heard he has since been joined by some person better calculated for such measures, and I hope it is so.

I presume Mr. Barnard will transmit to you the General's own accounts of what has passed since his departure, collected from his letters to Mr. Ross.[1] The only letter Mr. Barnard has had was to desire him to communicate to you the situation of things—a painful enough task, and one that Mr. Barnard regrets he must perform in a manner so very inadequate to what you must naturally expect from the situation he fills here. But he cannot help it. The General, I am grieved to say, neither consults him, nor permits any of his opinions to be advanced,

---

[1] Mr. Hercules Ross had acted as Secretary under General Craig. On Mr. Barnard's arrival he was appointed Deputy-Secretary with a alary of £1,500 a year.

without that silencing manner which renders a man fearful of subjecting himself to what it would be difficult to bear.

In one of my letters I gladly mentioned to you that I trusted and hoped that things would go on well, as Mr. Barnard had on occasion (I might have said occasions), where his respectability in the Colony was much compromised, remonstrated with the General in a manner so dispassionate and judicious, as to hit the General's temperate key. From what then passed, Mr. Barnard had good hopes that the General would rectify the unlucky habit of making him a cipher. Indeed, to such a point was this carried, that the Landdrost of Stellenbosch, etc., asked Mr. Barnard if he was any longer, except nominally, the Secretary to the Colony. Unfortunately his hopes soon vanished, despatches were received, annexed—all sorts of business done, without the General's even mentioning the facts to Mr. Barnard. You will therefore judge how little he has had to do with measures which are so generally reckoned here to have been incautious. I should grieve if you could suppose Mr. Barnard's counsels had any share in them, which you might be led to suppose from knowing the earnest manner in which Lord Macartney recommended him to the General, and even left it in his instructions that he was to take no steps without consulting them well over with him.

In this read my apology for having presumed to

take up your attention by my poor details on what is so much out of my walk as this war, its commencement, or duration. But I wish you to know privately from me, what I think Mr. Barnard's delicacy will spare you the knowledge of from himself, that he has all along in the most respectful manner, as far as he durst, marked his disapprobation, when any of the General's methods of going on appeared to him too hasty, or wanting in discretion. I do assure you, my best friend, that nothing but the solid gratitude Mr. Barnard feels for your kindness and patronage could have made him bear, as a man, the degraded situation in which the General's thoughtless want of all reference to him places him. But he looked upon his situation as Acting-Governor[1] to be one which would not last long; and he thought he could best mark his gratitude to you by avoiding the smallest dispute or quarrel with so near a relation of yours.

With all this, to feel any further resentment at the General than that of the moment is impossible. He is as God made him, an honest man, with many disinterested, manly, good points. I had once hoped that he was improved, from what he was originally made, by having lived longer in the world, but I see he is better calculated to do well under a good master than as the head.

[1] General Dundas was Lieutenant-Governor and Commander-in-Chief, but he was now Acting-Governor until Lord Macartney's successor should arrive at the Cape.

I suspect you think as we do here, by your sending out a new Governor at once. Your nephew, great as the employment is, might doubtless have filled it till the peace, if you had seen it proper, unless that is likely to be a very distant period.

Sir George Yonge's appointment [1] was one that at first surprised people here. A successor to Lord Macartney was looked for in the more brilliant class of ability than the world is apt to rank Sir George; but this apart, I am sure he will be received in such a manner as to please him. I am not well pleased with some of the English, who have been at pains to communicate his embarrassed situation to the Dutch, with no other view I believe but that of being witty and sneering—that bane of all conversation. We shall welcome him, despite this, with every attention to our shore. With joy I shall welcome Lady Yonge, too, if she comes, and offer her every civility in my power till she becomes the patroness of the place to show civility to me. All the little aid my experience can give she shall have.

It is with not a little satisfaction I can say at the end of the General's administration that it will

---

[1] Sir George Yonge was the only son of Sir William Yonge, Walpole's Secretary of State for War. He had experience of political and official life, and held important posts. He had been M.P. for Honiton, a Lord of the Admiralty, Vice-Treasurer of Ireland, Secretary for War, and Master of the Mint, which last office he held until February 1799, when he was appointed Governor of the Cape of Good Hope. His appointment was probably due to the King's influence, with whom he was a favourite. He was nearly seventy when he was appointed.

close without Mr. Barnard having had open rupture with him, and it is with satisfaction that we mean to invite a young lady who, we are told, comes out to become Mrs. 'General' Dundas. She shall remain with us if she will accept of the invitation till he returns to Cape Town, which is not expected to be by any means a near prospect. I know not how you approve of this invited wife, who braves the dangers of the seas to join him; but if she is a sensible, reasonable woman, whether possessed of a penny or not, I shall think the General will be the better for her.

With respect to Sir George and Lady Yonge, if they do me the honour of consulting me at all on their modes of life, as applicable to the Colony, I shall give them such hints as I think will conduce most to their own good, and the general happiness, as well as to the respectability of his station as Governor. This place is not wholly to be governed by wisdom, ability, or elevation of mind. There is a set of ways of thinking and prejudices amongst the residents which it is worth the while of a man and his wife who are placed at the head of affairs, and likely to remain here some time, to study. The Dutch, in particular, respect parade, and all sorts of high etiquette. So far from lowering the person who expects it in their eyes, it is only reckoned a proof of his being a great man. Sir George Yonge must wear a double row of gold lace on his coat to what Lord Macartney did, to sweep away the impressions given of his poverty; and as to Lady Yonge, I shall endeavour to set her up a gracious queen in every way, and shall be the first to bow down to her. There is no call for any extravagant expense to sustain the representation; they may easily save 5,000*l*. a year of their income, but representation will be well. If I do not forget the sort of woman I recollect to have heard Lady Yonge is, she will not dislike my advice. I have not taken my own advice, as I never gave way to parade. But my line was different from hers; the wife of the Secretary of the Colony has no call on her—what she does is her own free choice—no *devoir*; and I do not like nonsensical constraints or formalities, though I pay every attention to the duties of hospitality.

A word more respecting Kaffir Land, or rather the present scene of the war, before I finish. I hear that General Dundas begins to suspect that matters might have been better conducted at first, and is anxious to make peace with the Hottentots and Kaffirs, foreseeing no end to the war. I hear, too, that General Vandeleur thinks it also the best scheme, but that both have an idea of licking them first—and a very good idea it might be, if they would stand still to be licked. But as pitched battles are totally opposite to Kaffir modes of fighting, I hope the Generals won't count on one. I should imagine it is by verbal explanations, by presents to their chiefs, by the promise of protection and future justice to their Hottentots, that they will be more likely to succeed; and if the Dutchmen who have sheltered themselves amongst them, and are partly at the bottom of this, were to have promise of pardon and a *douceur* privately, I should think it might be useful. This is not a very noble plan, you will say; but people must fight with such weapons as are in their hands, if they are not indifferent about the event, or if the danger is great.

It is supposed, if the Kaffirs condescend to negotiate at all now, that they will stipulate to keep the part of the country they have lately pillaged. It is the richest, to be sure, and, along with part of their own and Gaika's territory, affords most of the cattle sent to the Cape. Any proposal of this sort on their part would probably be rejected *in toto*. Perhaps I am about to launch a very foolish idea. I have launched it by way of question in common conversation, and always found it hooted at, but I'll launch it to *you*, because I have often heard you say ' Speak out all your nonsense, Anne—I like to hear everybody's ideas.' Well, were we to give up to the Kaffirs that part of the country I mention, supposing they stipulate for it, and supposing that we can according to our treaty with the Dutch, where would be the harm? The farms are already plundered and destroyed, the implements of husbandry burnt. The cattle are 'lifted,' as they say in Scotland, and the farmers fled; nor will they dare to return unless their thinly scattered houses (for thinly scattered they are, in spite of its being the richest part of the Colony in our possession) are protected by one regiment or more, quartered so as to render each individual farm secure, and they are at a distance of about six miles from each other. It has generally been allowed in Cape Town that the Dutch settlements reach inconveniently far from the Cape; 800 or 1,000 miles is a long way to send our troops to guard a few farmhouses. Their motive in going originally so far was not because the lands nearer the Cape are not fit to raise grain, rear cattle, etc., but because every man wished to have a large range for his beasts, and the power of turning up new ground every year for his grain, one crop of which comes up well without manure and with little trouble.

If we gave up that country to the Kaffirs, which, by the bye, they *must* keep if they please, whether we give it up or not, and make the Boers a compensation by giving them portions of the unappropriated lands nearer the Cape, we should save further quarrelling, expense of men and money, have our grain and cattle much cheaper (as the heavy charge and much difficulty of land carriage would be saved), and be more collected together in case of future wars. The lands would be better cultivated, and cattle soon raised in large numbers. If we eat mutton in the meantime, of which there is plenty at an easy distance from the Cape, instead of beef, it will do us no harm. But if we make peace with the Kaffirs they will gladly furnish us as usual with cattle, in return for such articles as they want, and if, from time to time, they pillage our farmers at 200 or 300 miles' distance, the matter will be easier adjusted than if it was at 1,000 miles. If we cannot effect peace with them now, I sincerely hope we may withdraw our handful of men without thinking it necessary to fight longer. A better chance than our fighting is that the Hottentots and they may quarrel about the booty, or that Gaika may become jealous of them and attack them from behind. To retain *his* friendship at any price I fancy would be wise; was he to join the others, then indeed it would be time to think of departure. As to the Hottentots, my poor friends, whom, from having seen a good deal of, I am always disposed to say a word for, some military men have proudly said that if they lay down their arms and make peace unconditionally, it will be time enough to see justice done then. This may be very good doctrine in the Army or Navy, not to appear to be forced into anything, but the Hottentots are the free natives of the woods, and may stipulate for fair laws between them and the Dutch, and ourselves, and for justice in case of breach. If we had protected them sooner, and forced the Boers to be just and kind to them, I do not believe they would have turned against us now. They are of a timid, grateful nature, slowly roused to resent; but when they find the sweets of liberty I dare say they will value them. The original complaint the Boers made against

Fause, the Landdrost of Graaf Reinet, was that he was a favourer of 'heathens,' and had been known to sustain the Hottentot's cause against the Dutch master. Pardon, I dare say, might get those Hottentots back still, and new regulations bind them to us. In the Hottentot corps carrying the King's uniform they are steady to us (because we use them well) though brought against their countrymen.

That Sir George Yonge may be a Governor of peace, treading in all Lord Macartney's old footsteps, is the wish and hope of all here. This sounds like the ending of a sermon. I fear you will think it a very tiresome bit of reading, equally presumptuous and foolish; but all my aim is to give you what I know you like—Truth as far as I hear or know, although it may be at my own risk. We expect Sir George every day; our accounts are divided as to Lady Yonge's coming. When they arrive you shall have a short account of how they find us and how they like us. I will hope that the ladies will have a rather bad passage in order to make them prize the pleasures of dry land the more. All marriages, and the Cape follies of the day, in my next. God bless you.

XIII

The Castle, Cape of Good Hope:
November 8th, 1799.

I HAVE to acquaint you, my dearest Friend, of a melancholy event that took place the night of the 5th of November—the loss of the 'Sceptre.'[1] The gale which has lost us this poor old ship was one from the nor'-west, which rarely blows at this season of the year here; the wind was high, to be sure, but it was the heavy sea rolling in from the ocean on the beach which made it impossible for the ship to resist. The 'Sceptre' broke four cables, and five other ships which were lost were equally unfortunate, but their crews were saved. The 'Sceptre' we always understood to be a very crazy old ship, and one that would be broken up on coming home. The spectacle her wreck exhibited was melancholy to a degree; the pieces she was in being by the gale broken into such atoms as seemed fit only for firewood. Captain Edwards was a mild-mannered and well-esteemed man; he made it a constant rule, which he did not ever depart from after he had the command

[1] The 'Sceptre' went on shore in the gale, and Captain Edwards, his sons, some officers, and the greater part of the ship's company perished in the wreck.

here, of not sleeping on shore, and to this excellent rule he fell a worthy sacrifice. His son was with him—a fine boy of twelve years of age. His boy has been found, and in his bosom a prayer-book. Many, many more might have been saved than were saved, had they not been bruised in the water by the small pieces of the wreck. The beach was covered with people; fires were kept burning all night, and every assistance afforded that could be given. Mr. Barnard was there. Nothing could surpass the zealous humanity of Colonel Crawford, who loves a good sleep in a good bed as well as most people, but was up the greater part of the night, encouraging his old fellows of the 91st to do their best in saving the floating creatures. Nearly one hundred were saved. That is an honest good regiment, the men almost all infirm, but trusty. Another mutiny has been hatching in the 81st Regiment; again found out by privates in the 91st, and their officers put on their guard. What can be expected from Vinegar Hill boys? I suppose, when General Dundas returns from the war, some of the people concerned in it will be likely to suffer.

Our bay has of late been crowded with Danish vessels; their purpose seems rather equivocal. General Dundas being absent, no one has stepped forward to show them much civility. I except ourselves, as Mr. Barnard has frequently invited them here; they seem well-bred, plain men. On this late sad event, when the ship of the Danish

Commodore was lost (though the crew was saved), Mr. Barnard pressed him (and one or two of his first officers) to make this house his home while he remained at the Cape. A variety of reasons made him wish the Commodore to accept of this civility, which he presumed it politic as well as humane to offer; but the Commodore said that the Danish Consul had given them beds at his house, and they were too much occupied and agitated to be comfortable guests at present. The Collector of the Customs [1] offered them room for the accommodation of their things, if the Commodore would pledge himself and his word of honour that he had no goods on board but such as were not illicit. He did. He gave him his honour he had not; the question was a necessary one to put, and the firmness and boldness of the assurance to the contrary rather surprised us.

Nothing final yet from Graaf Reinet. Colonel Crawford has a letter to tell him that his Grenadiers are embarked and coming to the Cape, and a peace with the Kaffirs is negotiating. I am a little surprised at the men's coming away before it is concluded. I hope it will prove a lasting one; but in truth we have no expectation of it, as plunder is a better thing to a Kaffir or Hottentot than a peace he is to gain nothing by, and which he is only forced into by fear. I hope, if the General makes peace with them, he will settle something of the nature of annual presents to ensure its continuance. Unless

[1] Mr. John Hooke Green, who enjoyed a salary of 1,000*l.* a year.

there is a prospect of gain by behaving well now they certainly won't keep the peace, but will begin pillaging again whenever they conceive our force to be inferior to theirs. What a pity they were ever annoyed by forcing them out of a territory where they were doing no harm!

No Governor yet.

XIV

The Castle, Cape of Good Hope:
December 14th, 1799.

A SHIP sails to-morrow for St. Helena, by which I may have an opportunity of writing again to my dearest Friend, and here are two-thirds of this day gone already in nursing the sick. But I have something for my pains, as I have assisted in introducing into the world a little girl whom Mrs. Crawford was safely delivered of two hours ago, who, as the old nurse in 'Romeo and Juliet' says, will 'be the mother of boys hereafter.' I have therefore but a minute's time to say a thousand things. My heart is filled with a mixture of sensations which it is perhaps well for your patience that I have not leisure to develop. But upon the whole the pleasure of seeing your handwriting again addressed to myself, of reading that you are well, happy, though busy, that everything is 'prospering' in your hands, the pleasure of receiving long letters from dear Margaret and dear Lord Macartney, which, though they suspend a favourite hope, yet convey the disappointment in a manner by no means unflattering or unkind—all fill, agitate, expand, contract, yet on the balance, content my heart.

Our wish has then been fully expressed by Lord Macartney of our obtaining leave of absence to return home for a time, but you did not then choose to comply with it because you did not think you ought, as the face of affairs stood, and considering the period of our stay to have been then only two years. You say nothing on the subject yourself—I believe you grieve to hurt me by a denial; but you need not have feared it at this moment, my best friend, for had you given us the permission we should not at the present time have made use of it. The arrival of the new Governor gives Mr. Barnard a hope that his stay may really be of some use to the Colony. During General Dundas's administration his place has been a sinecure, owing to his neither having been trusted nor employed, but this I hope will soon cease. Be well assured, my best friend, that your approbation of his conduct hitherto, and the dependence you place on him for assisting in future councils, are such motives as would keep him here (and me along with him) cheerfully for any length of time almost, while his assistance appeared necessary.

Yet from time to time you must give me liberty (in the hope of being forgiven) to reiterate my wishes for discretionary liberty to Mr. Barnard to go home on leave for a time, which would carry us home by-and-by to pay a visit to our old parents, all of them past seventy, who fear they are never to see us again. Without Mr. Barnard I cannot go.

Contented and happy in my domestic life, under circumstances rather singular and not fairly assorted,[1] should I risk the future comfort of my advancing years for any other duty, or gratification to myself, by letting him find out that he can be happy without me, which at present he does not believe? No, no, my dear friend, the risk of breaking up such harmony would be too great to run. Give us, therefore, this leave, I pray, to come together, and trust to our limited circumstances, and to our being much liked in this Colony, for our returning. You said to my sister, as advice for her to transmit to us, that she should counsel us not to think of returning to England till we had made enough to render us a little more at ease in point of finance. But, my dear friend, recollect that though whatever we can save out of our salary, or lay up from our friends at home, is money to be counted on, beyond this there is not the possibility of advantage with either honesty or propriety of accumulating more. And this from the wise rules that you yourself made, abolishing all perquisites to those in office, which I rejoice in every day of my life. A little matter I think may be saved at home and here, in the course of our stay, after paying the expenses of living, and a few small old scores of Mr. Barnard's to no great amount; but it cannot be much. I shall tell you truly the sum, and as I am really an honest woman you may trust me. I shall add no more on this

[1] She alludes to the disparity of age.

subject except one word. You said to my sister that you would have been *ashamed* to have asked his Majesty so soon for leave for Mr. Barnard to go home. A twelvemonth from the time you said this I think you will blush the less. To his Majesty's goodness I am ready to trust, with such a friend as you to back the cause. He, the King, has as good heart as any man in his dominions, and as much consideration for others; show him some of the arguments I have used, and I am persuaded that, after an absence of four years from England, he will indulge us in a short visit to home.

Our new Governor, Sir George Yonge, arrived here about a week ago. I mentioned to you in my last that we had prepared excellent accommodation for him and all his suite, and for the ladies. We put up beds and procured every requisite necessary for their comfort, which it is well here to provide before they are wanted. Mr. Barnard had told Major Erskine (General Dundas's late *aide-de-camp* and friend) that we meant to request the company of Miss Cuming till his return. You may, therefore, suppose that we were both surprised and mortified when, on Mr. Barnard's accompanying the Commodore on board to pay an early visit to the new Governor, he found that Major Erskine had taken a boat, boarded the ship before she came to anchor, and had, in General Dundas's name, made a point of the Governor's going to a Dutchman's house in the first place (the future father-in-law of Major Erskine, as report says), and to Rondebosch next day, four miles out of Cape Town. Moreover, General Dundas requested that Miss Cuming might remain under his Excellency's care till the Government House, occupied by Lord Macartney and by himself afterwards, was ready for the Governor's reception. This arrangement did not seem to have been preferred by Sir George Yonge or by the ladies, but the Governor had given a hasty assent, and did not think he could retract. I was particularly sorry at it, as I had hoped to have begun a little friendship with Mrs. Blake[1] and Miss Cuming by the kindness I meant to show them, and I was surprised at my intention having been frustrated by Major Erskine, and in a manner that appeared too eager to have been accidental.

Next morning I waited on all at their lodging-house. Sir George received me like an old friend; he had told Mr. Barnard that I was one of his most esteemed friends and of longest standing. I was glad to hear it—who would not be even *Eve's contemporary* to be the friend of the First Man in the world—in Africa at least? But I own that I recollected his face at Court better than our friendship in private. I found that he had kept his health charmingly during the voyage; his *aides-de-camp*, secretary, his niece, and Miss Cuming, all were well.

[1] Mrs. Blake was the niece of Sir George Yonge, and her husband (who came out with the suite) was the new Governor's private secretary.

Mrs. Blake seemed rather a showy, pretty woman, desirous of pleasing, and being civil, which will be well.

Miss Cuming I did not see. She had been so much disappointed on her first arrival by finding General Dundas at so great a distance and engaged in war, that it had unfitted her for seeing anybody, and she declared she would not appear in public till his return. I thought her right. The less a woman in delicate situations exposes herself to animadversion the better. I had an amiable character of her from the captain of the ship she came in; I hope sincerely to find her deserving of it, as it will be of some importance to us all that she should be of the cementing quality which sweetness and sense can always be if they please. The paragraph in your letter regarding her I shall keep to myself. I cannot imagine why the General did not beg Lady Jane's protection and advice to her on her way to this arduous undertaking, and your sanction to the step. The independence of acting I do not think should have been exerted so fully on this occasion, for her sake. As to the paragraph which conveys your satisfaction of the General's conduct as far as you could judge of it to the end of August, and Lord Macartney's favourable report of, and interest in, him, I shall in justice to you and Lord Macartney transcribe it for the General. It is saying something for the liberality of my mind, and more for the interest I take in any 'favourite child' of yours (the Cape I know is one), when I assure you that I shall be better contented to be found wrong by you, and even scolded a little for having supposed some of the General's measures to have been rather injudicious, than that you should think they have essentially injured the tranquillity of the Colony. How soon he will be able to join his love we know not; peace and war are alternately talked of. Peace I am now convinced he wishes to make, but I doubt much if there will be a lasting one, unless the Kaffirs and Hottentots are kept true by the hope of further benefits.

Sir George and the ladies went to Rondebosch the day after their arrival, and have resided there ever since. A table is covered for eighteen every day, and a company of particular friends of the General and of Erskine are invited by Erskine to dine with the Governor. Mr. Barnard has never been invited there. He sees that, but he takes no notice of anything; he feels himself the natural friend of Sir George, the lawful wife of the Colony, and any little attempts made to injure him by the 'Dollys' he will undo, he hopes, at leisure, when Sir George fixes in town. Meantime Sir George is taken possession of by the Staff, and by their anxiety to keep Mr. Barnard at a distance I suppose they have some view in it which time will develop.

General Dundas continues to correspond with Mr. Ross and with General Fraser. A paragraph in a letter to the last named, which was shown to

Mr. Barnard, determined him to offer to the Governor now what he at first meant to have offered the General on his return. 'To be sure,' says General Dundas, 'the Government House in the Castle which Mr. Barnard occupies is the fit one for me as Commander-in-Chief. I gave it up to him only at Lord Macartney's request, but when Sir George Yonge arrives he will make what arrangements he pleases.' Mr. Barnard before this, as I mentioned, had determined to offer our house to the General on his marriage; it is the best house in the place next to that the Governor occupies, and the Lieutenant-Governor's giving it up to us when he had no wife is a reason why Mr. Barnard was glad to put it again in his hands, when he was beginning *un état* where a little additional representation might not perhaps be either disagreeable to him or to her. Mr. Barnard therefore took an early opportunity to tell Sir George that the house was at his service to offer to General Dundas, if he preferred it to his own house in the Castle. He told me that Sir George appeared as if a millstone had been untied from his neck. 'I am very much obliged to you, sir,' he replied, 'very much indeed; I never could have asked you to give up your house, but I believe the General wishes for it, and since you are so good as to offer it to me, I beg you may rather have the merit of offering it to himself.' This Mr. Barnard declined. The General has behaved too unkindly to us to render it now natural for Mr. Barnard to pay him a compliment, though our attachment to his uncle would lead us to give him up cheerfully every point of public pre-eminence which he is entitled to. Sir George went on to tell Mr. Barnard that he should not be a loser by this conduct, as he should certainly make him a handsome allowance for a house in town. This Mr. Barnard utterly declined. He did not think Government ought to be put to any new expense on his account. Sir George said he could easily manage that. But I am certain Mr. Barnard never will accept of any compensation which puts Government to a new expense, particularly as he sees a tendency to spending money rashly, which he could not be authorised by respectful hints to restrain, if the first act of Sir George's administration was to confer an apparent obligation on himself. While Government has any other house to bestow, little or large, situated so that he may fulfil the duties of his office, he will have no allowance for one, nor even then, unless authorised by you. So much for the little politics of our Lilliput court.

How our new folks will like the Cape I know not. I dare say the *aides-de-camp* won't, at least one of them, Colonel Cockburn,[1] as I hear he is a little of a fine gentleman, and they, you know, are despisers by trade. Sir George, I think, must be happy. He will like the sort of life a Governor has it in his power to lead. For my share, I think the

[1] Principal *aide-de-camp* to the Governor, who was greatly under his influence.

transition from debt and Holyrood House to being his Excellency here, and looked up to by everything but the Table Mountain, is such a one as requires the snow of sixty-three years at least to stand. As to the ladies, I hope they will have their share of happiness, from being made goddesses of in their different ways. I at first regretted that Lady Yonge had not come. I am a good subject, and apt to think that one supreme Queen Bee is better than any chance of a divided hive. I hope there won't be any, as both of our new ladies are reckoned good-humoured, though from some little things which have dropped from the friends of the one or the other I should not be surprised if they were distinct powers, and that I, instead of being poor little Holland, ready to be swallowed up by everybody, may chance to represent the Armed Neutrality, and, like old England, while I am the least, be greatest, by possessing in my hands 'the balance of power.' But I must not talk nonsense. Good-bye.

XV

The Castle, Cape of Good Hope:
January 5th, 1800.

Imprimis. My dearest 'Friend'—Dare I say it?—our new Governor, I fear, is a very, very weak old soul. He is full of good intentions and great intentions, but how his acts will turn out I am not sure. He is disposed to conceive that he is the man who is to make this a fine and flourishing Colony; that no one else at home was thought equal to that task; that nothing as yet has been done. He does not perceive the wisdom of our late Governor (I mean Lord Macartney) in pausing over all measures which were likely to disburse the public money till he was sure the Cape was to remain with us, while he permitted no wise regulation which cost nothing to remain undigested, or established. On the contrary, Sir George Yonge is for having every supposed improvement done at once, and I fear does not begin with the things most necessary, but with those most connected with his own domestic conveniency. To Mr. Barnard he is hearty, apparently open, and very flattering in his expressions. He wishes to take credit with him (for what I trace to you through the good opinion of Lord Macartney) of connecting Mr. Barnard by some document in writing with himself and the Lieutenant-Governor in the Councils to be held in future on public measures. This is a testimony of *your* opinion of him which I own myself very particularly glad of, for various reasons, some of which I trace every day more clearly to their source. Sir George says that *he* requested you to put Mr. Barnard in that document. Mr. Barnard has not seen what he alludes to, but he has an idea of its nature. It will give him the right of speaking out his mind, and of remonstrating with respectful firmness where he thinks it necessary, and ultimately of expressing his opinion in writing when he cannot influence, which he has reason to think may be the best way both with the Governor and the Lieutenant-Governor, for different reasons. But before we come to grave matters let us have a little chat on slight things.

After a week's residence at Rondebosch, the Governor and his family returned to town and to the house of Mynheer du Val, where they slept, while the daytime was spent at the Government House in overseeing reparations, improvements, and unpacking of furniture. The Governor has a great love of pretty things of that sort. I could have told him that less carving, and black morocco leather instead of scarlet, would have suited the Cape better; but it is needless to put people out of conceit with what they have got. If Sir George Yonge will superintend the reparation of the public buildings falling to decay (as they do here in a twelve-month's time almost, if not attended to, so rapidly do the rains pierce and burst the clay walls), as well as he superintends the reparation of his own kitchen, he will be a treasure. But as a Governor is not quite in his place doing so, I don't expect that. To build a new staircase in the Government House was his first plan, to repair the Government gardens and build a high wall all round them the second. Other plans came forth which I shall mention in their place. Mr. Barnard trembled for the wall—it would not have cost less than 2,000 rix dollars (needlessly laid out)—so he got it undermined—at least he has procured a delay, and that he looks on as nearly the same thing. The staircase he tried to influence into an alteration only. It really is necessary, being so narrow and perpendicular in the steps that nothing short of Lord Macartney's resolution to do nothing, and the beautiful thing called *habit* which accustomed him to hop up like a parrot to his perch, would have made it practicable for a person with a gouty tendency to mount it. The separation of the Government gardens Sir George began directly, and, planting guards at the gates, refused entrance to the inhabitants till the Governor's gardens should be put in order. Had he torn the Magna Charta of the Cape into a thousand tatters he could not have put the Dutch into such an alarm. For 150 years they had enjoyed the privilege of walking under the shade of those oaks—'tis the only public walk at the Cape—and all ranks of people, the women particularly, were furious. Mr. Barnard heard of the manœuvre, and knowing the sort of effect this would have (which the civility of ten revolving years would not have the power to wipe away), he hurried off with a proclamation in his pocket, undoing the restriction by leaving the main walk free while the others were repairing. Sir George kept the paper; but when he sent it back, though he adopted much, he had introduced a foolish rule to make all persons write down their names every time they enter the gardens (which they do sometimes a dozen of times in a day) in a book at the guard-house. They think it a great trouble. This is a way of making private property of a public benefit.

After we had waited, as in duty bound, till General Fraser, our Commander-in-Chief in General Dundas's absence, had given the first dinner to the Governor, we invited him here, also Sir Roger Curtis,[1] the Staff, and the heads of departments, etc.—a dinner of thirty people. In the evening I had my Thursday party, and, being desirous to influence the future invitations of Sir George by

---

[1] Vice-Admiral and Commander-in-Chief of the Fleet at the Cape of Good Hope (on the death of Sir Hugh Christian) from 1799–1801. He was a distinguished naval officer, and afterwards became Commander-in-Chief at Portsmouth.

showing him a company composed of many of those who are attached to Government, I wrote notes to many of the most democratic of my Beauties and their families, saying that, as the new Governor and his family were to be with us in the evening, I wished to present my old friends to the new. The effect was all I could desire—everyone came, and I had a splendid assembly. Sir George fell directly in love with the daughter of one of the greatest Jacobins in the place, as it was once supposed, though it has otherwise proved, and flirted as if he had been twenty-five. On the other hand, having observed, as I told you before, that there was a strong tendency amongst the higher military powers to exclude the subordinate officers from all share in pleasant dances or parties, I hinted to the colonels to bring all their ensigns and lieutenants, that they might appear in one civil house by way of a precedent, if that was anything. They thanked me and came. Of course, there was a handsome company, and as many supped as could find chairs. I presented my Dutch ladies to the Governor, and to his niece, Mrs. Blake. They were surprised at their number and smart appearance.

The Thursday after, Mr. Barnard invited fifty-six of the principal Dutchmen to meet the Governor and the Admiral. The Staff also, of course, all came. I again secured my ladies, and, having foreseen that there would be a great deal of company, I had a sly provision of fiddlers ready to give Mrs.

Blake an impromptu ball. Miss Cuming, I was sorry, was not of the party; she does not go out yet. The ball, being unexpected, went off charmingly. Mr. Barnard set Mrs. Blake a-going, and Sir George had his little lassie again to flirt with. As to Sir Roger Curtis, in all secrecy be it spoken, he says that, now as General Dundas is to be wed, as Admiral he reckons a flirtation with Mrs. Baumgardt[1] is attached to his Flag. Mrs. Baumgardt is perfectly of the same opinion. She is a good-humoured, vain creature, and a very good mother to her children, though she certainly does make fish of one and flesh of another. Her husband finds no fault, so 'tis no business of anybody's. A quiet little Englishwoman (Mrs. Pattison) whispered to me as at supper the two gentlemen were ogling their loves: 'How do you think Lady Yonge and Lady Curtis would like it, if they were to see their old boys behaving so?' Jesting apart, for this is only a jest as yet, I don't see what they can do but coquet! If wives won't accompany honest men they must run the chance. Sir Roger seems to be a clever, pleasant man, and I hear he is an excellent officer.

I believe this is the last party we shall ever have in this house. There has been much shabby manœuvring going forward which has now explained itself, but I trust that temperance, silence, and proper dignity, never asserted till the moment is ripe, will put all things to rights in a little time.

[1] Wife of one of the judges of the High Court of Justice.

Without orders from the Governor, General Fraser has moved into General Dundas's house in the Castle. Without orders, Major Erskine has taken possession of General Fraser's. They have circulated it everywhere, that Mr. Barnard has received the Governor's commands 'to move off and to make way for General Dundas'; and as they conceive this to be a pretty broad hint, they wonder he does not take it, the more so as they have flitted their furniture before our windows into their new houses.

Sir George at last is displeased; they have fortunately trodden on his toes, while they were meditating only a triumph over Mr. Barnard. Major Erskine invited him into 'his house' yesterday, when Sir George was in the Castle yard. 'I did not know this was *your* house, sir.' 'Oh yes; General Fraser has gone to live in General Dundas's late house, and that makes room for me.' 'Humph. I beg, sir, to have the pleasure of seeing you at two o'clock to-day, and General Fraser at the same hour.' He passed on. 'Don't stir,' said his Excellency to Mr. Barnard; 'make no move—this is a little *too* much.' Mr. Barnard said he did not mean to move till he had the Governor's orders. The truth is it had been settled by the gentlemen who at present try, as Sir George says, 'to have all their own way,' that *we* were to leave the Castle and to have no Government house at all, but an allowance for a house, which was to be that of Mr. du Val, father to Major Erskine's intended, and also to a fair lady who smiles on General Fraser. General Dundas was not only to have our house, but was to keep Rondebosch, it being convenient for the horses of the Staff to eat the barley its gardens produce. They had almost persuaded the Governor to put *all* the public offices, the bank, etc. (at present secure and within one court) out of the Castle too. His Excellency threw out a hint of this to Mr. Barnard, saying that Mr. Pitt had them all near himself, and that he was a very great man. 'A very great one indeed,' said Mr. Barnard, 'but, Sir George, the Cape is not England, nor this place the town of London. The expense of getting other offices would far exceed any benefit that the change could be of; at least pause till you can look about you.' This was agreed to, but the idea of Mr. Pitt's having all public offices within a step of Downing Street is not out of his head yet.

I do not think my old friend Henry Dundas would turn me out of doors without giving me another door to enter, if he were here; money we won't take. One of Sir George's family, who came to like Mr. Barnard particularly, at a dinner lately, where there was a small company and a little of the *in vino veritas* which very good claret produces, said in Mr. Barnard's ear, 'Do you see anything going forwards at our house?' 'A little,' said Mr. Barnard. 'The truth is,' replied the other, 'that certain gentlemen who have taken possession of us, have moved heaven and earth to prejudice Sir

George both against you and Lady Anne, but they have shot their bolt in vain. Have patience—though they influence at present, things will come round by-and-by. Keep my secret and profit by it with discretion.' What may be drawn from all this? Exactly this. Madame Human Nature is the same all the world over, whether she is man or woman, whether dressed in scarlet or blue. I might have seen from the first that *one* description of men—the Staff men in this garrison—have been envious of Mr. Barnard. Living in the very centre of the Castle, in the best house, with the best salary, with a sort of little *éclat* from the accident of having a wife to whose train a 'Ladyship' is pinned, they have been jealous of him. Not the thousand civilities and kindnesses we have done them, nor the good dinners they have been constantly receiving from us, have been of any other use than to make them the more angry at his powers of giving them better dinners than they could return. General Dundas of himself would not have behaved to us quite as he has done, had it not been for a set of men inferior to himself, who have disliked Mr. Barnard for no other cause than what I am mentioning. They have considerable sway over the General, but so long as Lord Macartney remained the consideration in which *he* held Mr. Barnard awed their attempts. He gone, the day was theirs. All this has had no effect beyond their own circle. There is not, I will venture to say, an officer in this garrison or a civilian in the Colony (those connected with the Staff excepted) who has not the most perfect respect as well as affection for Mr. Barnard. He is literally the 'honest man's friend'; the Staff only make a foe of him, though a foe he will not condescend to suppose he is made.

I have seen Miss Cuming frequently since I began this letter. She is not handsome; but if her qualities are real, her temper good, and her sense equal to the undertaking, I see nothing in her manner to prevent her being liked. I try to cultivate her; she is not cold to me, nor the contrary, which is just what I would have her to be to so new an acquaintance. I do not like over-eagerness in people to please—it generally falls off, and produces disappointment.

A new Hottentot chief is arrived in Cape Town with a face of a different character from any I have seen before—finely made. Mr. Barnard is taking him to the Governor, who said he wished to receive him with 'some state,' and asked me what sort of cold collation he would like. I told him a good lump of boiled beef or mutton, and a little brandy, but begged his French cook might not put any of his *savoir faire* into the mess; those people don't like anything high—they don't even eat salt if they can avoid it. One of the chief's train has a curious instrument, which I am convinced might make a man's fortune in England, so I have bought it of him for 2s.—a stick with a peg and a bit of sheep's gut, which he applies to his lips with a strong exertion from the lungs, and produces a sound as loud as any trumpet. He played the dragoons' music, and told me he could learn anything I could teach him by singing. I think when I return I'll bring him in my suite! I have not heard anything more of peace or war. I hope we shall have the first, and that no extraordinary calls of any kind may demand further cash from our poor Treasury, which I fancy must be nearly penniless. What with 50,000*l*. which the Kaffir war must have cost at least, what with Sir George Yonge's salary for the last year, of 10,000*l*., and what with General Dundas's for the same year of 10,000*l*. (the third quarter of which he very properly did not draw for, as part of the fourth quarter had not expired when Sir George arrived, but all of which the Governor has made him a present of from the public funds), I fancy much new expense should be precluded for some time. Yesterday a person dined here, whom Mr. Barnard was very sorry to see at the Cape, though glad to offer him an abode in this house had he not been otherwise engaged, as he is a clever and honest man—the Governor of Batavia. He has unluckily come away at a time when it would have been fortunate had he stayed, but he had left the place before the news had reached it of the probable conquest of Holland. This man has by ability and good temper kept the Prince of Orange's flag flying for five or six years over the heads of a most Jacobin garrison. I fear he has not left a Governor as clever as himself, but the Fiscal seems to hope that he will prove true also.

Our Governor sent to beg a consultation with me on a ball he meditates giving two days after the Queen's Birthday. He wished me to draw the line of invitation. I recommended all the garrison and every Dutch person who had been in the habit of attending the *levées* or balls in the Dutch time, which is making them draw their own line. I know the folk here are critical respecting rank, and proud to a great degree. Some of my best female friends are the daughters of a butcher, John Van Rhenin, but they would disdain to be placed at table with another butcher, who sells the ox dead which their father sells alive. Some objections being made to my plan by a Dutch friend I highly respect, I closed with him on the point of making out the invitations to the wives and families of all who had been at the Governor's *levée* the first day of the year. I thought this was a way of keeping the door open to all future repentant sinners who might pay their compliments on future *levée* days, and afterwards be invited. Sir George is disposed to conciliate all; but I perceive some of the Dutch are eager to keep off others of their countrymen by calling them Jacobins. Now, among the whole of the people here, I look upon the best friends of Government to be only a set of men who have by accident fallen sooner than the others on what was for their interest; for as to foreseeing anything in this strange change of events, not even Mr. Pitt and you together, I dare say, could have pronounced finally on what the event of anything was to be. Now that all is going well with England and with the Dutch, some of them are anxious (as they prize attentions to themselves in proportion as they are denied to others) to keep other people at a distance, who might put in for a share of the loaves and fishes. These very people Mr. Barnard and I wish to have some civility paid to. Sir George is newly arrived, and need not enter into past or old politics. 'To be sure,' says my friend, 'they will all gladly come in now that they see the French game is up for them; but is that not very hard on *us*, to see ourselves at the same table with a set of rascals who would have overturned us all if they could?' 'That may possibly,' said I, 'hurt the pride of an individual, and what you say may be all very just, but Sir George has the instructions of his Court to show general civility. You will not find the enemies of Government treated in private with the consideration and confidence of its known friends.' I thought it was best to lay this general system of urbanity on your backs at home, to prevent their backs being up at Sir George. I believe nothing but my being a very great favourite would have made some of them pardon me for having introduced so many Jacobin Beauties as I did t'other night to Sir George. But I know that in all families women have their sway, and papa comes gently round to visit in the house where his *yonge vrows* are taken notice of.

I hear that at the *levée*, which was crowded, the Governor endeavoured as much as he could to talk, stand, think, look like his Majesty, in some of which points he succeeded to a certain degree. He wishes to make his ball like 'a certain one,' he told me, and hinted at St. James's. I fear the two rows of chairs round the room will constitute the only likeness. I said in my last that we would recommend representation to Sir George as agreeable to the Dutch. Perhaps you fear this advice may agree too much with his natural taste, and influence him to expense and folly. There is no call for either. Representation on public days is well here; if attention is also paid on private days to the business of the individual, and easiness of access is joined, a Governor will then be both feared and loved. Lord Macartney was respected and loved without parade; Sir George needs more, for he is not Lord Macartney. Oh no—no! He was repeating a conversation to me he had held with a Dutchman of consequence. 'I told him,' said he, 'that to good people this should be found a mild government.' 'Your Excellency is right,' said I. 'But to bad people it shall be a firm one,' he added. 'Your Royal Highness says justly' (I was very near replying). 'Firm,' cried he, darting out his arm and cocking his eyebrow. 'Firm—firm.' 'Oh, your Majesty is certainly right !!!'

January 12*th*, 1800.—I am sorry that I shall not be able to send you the sequel of what is now pending about our abode, as General Dundas cannot return, I find, for some days yet, and the ships sail to-morrow. I should have been glad to have been able to say whether I am 'a man or a mouse,' for his decision governs our motions, and makes me the lady of the Castle, or of Rondebosch, as he pleases, unless, when he makes his choice of the houses, he says, like a certain bishop—I forget whom, 'Baith's best.' In which case I shall live in a wee wee cottage Mr. Barnard is building, 'Paradise' being too old and crazy to be safe any longer, and Mr. Barnard will have to ride in every day at eight to his office, which I dare say the Staff will contrive to get shoved out of the Castle somehow.

Oh never, never have I felt the delay of leave of absence in the manner I do now. Never, I am sure, while I had the idea that our stay at the Cape might do good. But now I have only too much reason to fear that there is a party too strong establishing itself against us at the Government House, and I tremble for the ensuing twelvemonth. If Mr. Barnard is improperly treated by the Governor, in league with the General, I really fear he will throw up the game, and, along with me, prefer a turnip-top where we are loved and respected, to a life of oppression and spite shown us by the one side and endured in silence by the other. We are not people who can gossip and tittle-tattle—all must be on broad ground, or—sea and resignation. But be assured, my best friend, nothing shall be rashly or testily done. Better prospects may open, and gladly shall we embrace them. Still, still, if we can benefit a cat, do good to a human creature, or follow up your wishes particularly to your satisfaction, we will endure, even with the leave of absence in our pockets. Support us, however; we need it, and look to you for it. Forgive me. 'Out of the abundance of the heart the mouth speaketh.'

XVI

The Castle, Cape of Good Hope
February 7th, 1800.

IF you did not combine a great many other things to me with that of being a great man, I should make you a thousand apologies for my last letter, before I go on with this. It was full of female detail, full of those (only supposed) motives for conduct in others which vexed me, and it finished, I remember, agitated, oppressed, and imploring you to stand by us, else we were likely to be overpowered and trampled on by a strong party who were taking advantage of the weakness of our old Governor. How all this will *end*, I cannot yet say; perhaps I may see daylight in it before the next ships sail. At any rate, I will go on bringing up my account of things, so that a few words may finish my letter when a fair opportunity of sending it off occurs. If you tire of me, or blame me for troubling you with the *minutiæ* of things, recollect that it is to you alone that I open my heart; that your approbation is to us all in all in our present situation, and that in order to do ourselves justice I must let you behind the curtain.

I wrote to you that our Governor was to give a

great dinner on the Queen's Birthday, and a large ball the Monday following. To give fair play to his cooks, we proposed that he should dine with us the day before his dinner, to which he agreed. I hardly expected Miss Cuming would be of the party, as she had not dined out, and was the more surprised and pleased when she came. I hoped it was a desire of living in friendship with me, but as I thought perhaps a little curiosity to see this same house which had been so much talked of might mix, I showed her the whole after dinner—the fine pond in the back court, the view from the roof, and the number of bed-chambers, that she might judge of the conveniency of her premises to be. As it quite satisfies me, I was surprised to hear afterwards, and not sorry, that she did not like it at all. The bed-chambers, to be sure, are all paved with tiles, no wooden floors above stairs, but then they are spacious.

Meantime General Dundas wrote that he would arrive on Tuesday morning and marry the lady directly a peace was made with the Kaffirs and others. Of course we expected that Monday night she would spend in her own room, saying her prayers; a little anxious on a thousand points which a four years' absence from her lover might justify, and too much agitated to be fit for company. I leave *you* to settle from what cause she appeared at the ball, however, and danced away all night, when she was to be married next morning; and you shall also settle why, when the clergyman and the General arrived (the wedding taking place on the Wednesday), she would not come to be married, but ran off, wept, and made great difficulty. The weeping I thought not unnatural; one may cry from *attendrissement* as well as sorrow. There is also something imposing in a ceremony which agitates the nerves; but the running away I did not comprehend. Sir Roger Curtis, however, said it was 'All very right.' She was prevailed on at last; the marriage took place, and they went off to Rondebosch immediately.

There let us leave them for a day or two, and talk of some officers who came down from Algoa Bay, Graaf Reinet, etc.

As there is a good deal of variety of account given of that part of the country, I thought it not amiss to ask half a dozen of them, separately, what sort of country it really was which had been plundered; and what sort the part was from which General Dundas had ordered General Vandeleur to drive the Kaffirs. They told me it was admirable pasture country, no corn, called Brunches' Hook, or some name like that. All united in saying that the first 400 miles after leaving Cape Town were barren, sandy, unfertile (I cannot help thinking from being uncultivated), unwooded, and ill watered—the hollow brooks, which do not deserve the name of rivers, being all dry in summer, and the grounds parched up by the heat of the sun, except immediately on the banks of those brooks. This seems to be the reason why all the Dutch settlers agree in skipping over this part of the country. Not one of them has ever thought of digging to find water, and yet I have lately seen a variety of instances where this attempt, always laughed at as vain by the Boers and inhabitants here, has been attended with constant success. I am convinced this country is full of springs. I wish we had Lady Millbanke here to twist her wand for them; in that case Saldane Bay would soon, I dare say, become the capital of this country. We purchased a bit of ground some time ago; it went cheap from there being no water on it. A hasty low brook ran deep by the edge of it, almost dry in summer. Mr. Barnard, confident of success, built a cottage on it, where we shall live if we have no Government house allowed us, and in the centre of the kitchen, which is a white sandy soil, but rich beneath, while digging for clay for the walls, up popped a spring, which, having remained there for six months, I do not think will now get dry. The Dutch stare, and think we are very lucky; this bit of ground has always been reckoned good for nothing for want of water. Sir Roger Curtis too, enclosing a piece of ground on the sea-shore for a dockyard, found a fresh spring a foot or two beneath the surface, and within the sea-mark.

At Graaf Reinet the officers all allow that the soil becomes more moist and fertile. There is good pasture too, but inferior to what it is at Algoa Bay, and far inferior to the more remote districts. In these they described the vegetation to be luxuriant;

the grass better than the best field of grass in England, because taller and more of it; that their horses and cattle fattened and grew frisky upon it immediately; that there was plenty of large timber there, not in the glens only, as at Swellendam and at Sweet Milk Valley, but on the plains; trees feathered down to their roots like old English oaks, and clover breast-high, near which, however, it was dangerous for the troops to pass, for fear of serpents rushing out on them, whose sting is sometimes mortal, though less frequently so than in Bengal. They planted potatoes here, that best of fruits, but they ran all to leaf from the richness of the soil, and had nothing at their roots. The return of grain is frequently here a hundred and fifty fold. I must try to get you a little of various sorts for Dunira.[1] Cattle and sheep were there in plenty. General Vandeleur told me that while he paid the expense of the troops under his command, previous to General Dundas's arrival with the commissary department, the men could live on half their allowance, a sheep being only six dollars. He does not think the peace with the Kaffirs will last—no one does. He said he had pointedly followed his instructions during the first part of the war by attacking them, but I saw he wished it had been let alone. The latter part—namely, a peace made before they were conquered, after having been roused—he much disapproved of, together with the terms of that peace, and General Dundas's having

[1] Dundas's place in Perthshire.

granted them a new boundary, which was only winked at before. On these two points I, who am the worst of all judges to be sure, and always ready to cede much for peace, am more disposed to think General Dundas right than General Vandeleur. The person grants but little for peace who grants what will be kept whether granted or not. General Vandeleur says, that in all savage nations peace after hostility is only secured by fear, and General Dundas with 800 men might safely have attacked and subdued them, since he with less than 200 stood his ground, though the force was insufficient for dislodging them from the country they occupied.

As to all that, I do not believe they ever would have stood a regular engagement. I believe attempting it would have only prolonged a war which has tended to no good purpose, and I am therefore of the opinion of the poet who says ''tis the first wisdom, to be wrong no more.'

I hear the two Generals are not on good terms, but I hope not bad enough for it to be laid before *you*. General Vandeleur has fortunately got back his orders and papers, which the Kaffirs had possessed themselves of when they killed his servant. The chief of the band wears the wheels of the servant's watch in his ears by way of earrings. But what shall we say of my humble friends the Hottentots? One man only of that corps deserted, though they were brought against their countrymen. The officers describe them as the most faithful, disciplined, and obedient creatures in the world. A band of the servants of the Boers who joined the English certainly were afterwards ready to betray them, supposing they could not stand their ground. But in spite of this, General Vandeleur holds the Hottentot character to be good, and (where well treated for such a length of time as to inspire confidence) attached to a great degree.

I can perceive, however, from things in the newspapers and in letters from England, that there is a good deal of mistake about the number of Hottentots still existing in this country. I fancy that it is believed there are from 10,000 to 20,000, but, from what I can learn from those qualified to judge, I doubt much if there are above 4,000. 5,000 was the number mentioned to me, and I am afraid they are diminished since. There is now no longer any fixed territory for these poor people, except the vicinity of the missionaries,[1] where there are not above 300. The rest are all servants in the Colony, or live in small bands, establishing their kraals where they think they will be least annoyed, and ready to move off when they are so. The many other tribes which are to be found on piercing into this vast continent have each their fixed boundary, but the character of the tribes differs as much as their countenances and size do; a Bushman being ingenious, subtle, and faithless, as a Hottentot the contrary. The Kaffirs are a superior race in size, force, and judgment, I fancy, to either.

[1] The Moravian Settlement at Genadendal.

Jacob van Rhenin, a Dutch friend of mine, whom I have told you of before, in an account of our tour, started an opinion to me which, as it is curious and certainly not without some foundation, I shall repeat. Jacob is convinced, from conversations which he had with the natives when exploring the country to find the crew of the 'Grosvenor' many years ago, that the Kaffirs whom we have lately been at war with met the English troops with less fear because they believe them to be 'Men of the Sea'—that is, men, born and bred in vessels, leading a wandering life, without fixed habitation anywhere, poor, weak, and miserable. Vessels which have been wrecked on their coast have established this notion in them, as the crews have always appeared objects of pity, and begging for mercy. From this cause the Kaffirs have got the habit of despising these 'men of the sea,' who, from their spies sent to the Cape, they find have now got the Colony from the Dutch, and rule it with a 'wise old man' for their Governor—now, alas! gone away. General Dundas, I suppose, they must have reckoned a 'man of the sea' only, else they would have run from him. But I hope they will now look at Sir George Yonge's star, which shines brighter than Lord Macartney's did, and suppose him at once older, greater, and wiser than he.

To return to private matters. While General Dundas remained in the country with his new wife, General Fraser, Major Erskine, and the rest of that set, continued to press the Governor to order us out of the Castle, stating that the General wished very much he would, to save him the awkwardness of doing it when he came to town for the winter (this is February, the middle of summer). This hint Sir George totally resisted. He declared his intention of waiting the General's reply to his offer; and as the General seemed in no hurry to give it, the suspense became in some respects inconvenient, and in others unpleasant to us. Mrs. Dundas, I heard, much preferred Rondebosch to the Castle; and the General did so too—for the *summer*. It is cool, convenient as to offices, and has a most beneficial farm round it, at the moderate distance of four miles of good road from Cape Town. For us to have *no* Government house at all, after a three years' residence in one, would be very mortifying. The pecuniary loss I do not either name or think of when compared to the appearance it would have to the Dutch, who look at such things in men of public situations. It would tally too much with various malicious reports of our Staff friends, who have endeavoured to convince the Dutch, and all others who would listen, that no gratitude is due to Mr. Barnard or me for the pains we are at to entertain and to please them, as we are paid by Government for every ball and dinner we give, and have been allowed, while General Dundas was a single man, to occupy the Governor's house for that purpose. This would be a little provoking, if I cared much about what was said by those I do not esteem; but it is a shabby way of apologising for the want of those civilities in themselves, to say we have been paid for those we show. Most undoubtedly it is the salary of Government which pays for all we do, but so does the salary of every other servant of Government, and I never heard it hinted after you had given an excellent dinner at Wimbledon, or Mr. Pitt one in Downing Street, that you only kept eating-houses for the benefit of the State!

Meantime, we perceived from some little words that dropped first from one, then from another of the Government House people, that the old clique had been pressing their powers too far, and had begun already to jar with the new.

Already it popped out that the Government House people were half sorry that general invitations had been given to two or three gentlemen, who made their table an every-other-day conveniency, and whose company they began to find dull and censorious. All this we saw, and smiled at, pleased to find they were cutting their own throats, and pleased to draw no weapons whatsoever against them but those of good humour, cold chickens, music, and what little agreements this house could afford. The Governor, of course, was asked to our little evening parties with his household, etc. 'How cheerful and gay you are!' said he, 'and yet I never hear *you* abusing anybody! Pray let me see you as often as you can at my house; every night there a Scotch tray walks in at nine; it is an invention of the Advocate's, and holds twelve friends—all friends, mind me, we must sit too close for foes.' To this Scotch tray we have since often adjourned, and when we enter, off move the other party, who appear to be vanishing away one by one.

With respect to more important matters, Mr. Barnard and I begin to hope (nothing further having been done or proposed *en grand* by the Governor) that his little follies will not grow up to be greater ones. He has provided for his suite perhaps rather too liberally, and the department under the barrack-master is perhaps needlessly swelled by clerks and secretaries; but as this is a matter which regards his household and cannot occur again, it goes to no more than to so many unnecessary hundreds per annum. Mr. Barnard has frightened him a good deal about the revenue of the Colony being possibly unequal to the demands on it unless he is careful, and hinted that should it fail, the where to apply next is not pointed out. He thinks this had effect—in particular there is no longer any talk of a new set of public offices got, or more barracks built. Let them repair the old ones first, which need it much; old they are not, being scarcely finished when the Cape was taken.

We had a Botany Bay captain dining with us t'other day. I beg its pardon, by the bye, for I find Botany Bay takes it ill to be so called; New South Wales is its name. He is carrying a freight of bullocks from Cape Town—about 200. Mr. Hogan, a merchant here, tells me they cost Government 150*l.* each before they land them there, and that he has lately had a contract with it for a few which he put on shore at 36*l.* each, and that a merchant here can afford to do it much cheaper than Government can for itself. This I repeat, because you like to hear everything out of which any useful hint can be picked. There was no idea that I should repeat it, as it occurred only in common conversation. The captain of the ship, whose name is Kent, gave me a very pleasing account of Botany Bay (I beg its pardon again), and the reformation it works on individuals, most of whom become honest members of the community. He talks of Barrington with enthusiasm; of his good conduct, his modesty; his ability and public virtue are now, he says, as conspicuous as he was before conspicuously eminent in roguery. Though his time has been long up, he does not mean to return to Europe, but has a humble pride in being the First Magistrate where he is respected, instead of being pointed at at home, where he can never be forgotten in his first character. He was lately taken ill. All ranks of rogues, rogues of two years, three years, six years, and those made honest again by the sweeping clause of seven, bewailed him. He left all he had (about 1,500*l.*) to the orphans of the place. But he recovered, much to the satisfaction of the Governor.

I often say that I should have much pleasure, if

I were not a terrible coward, in going to Botany Bay and America before I return to England; but it would be feeling as an angel would to prefer a visit to Botany Bay to seeing my friends. The angels have more joy, it is said, over one sinner who repents, than over ninety-nine righteous persons. When I am put to the trial, however, with the leave of absence, I believe I shall prove myself a mere mortal woman, and sail home as fast as I can.

Governor King[1] and his wife were here on their way to New South Wales; good people, I think, and apparently well suited to their destination. I have seen them but twice, and that in this house. I sent a present of a silk gown to a rogue there, transported by Margaret and me; the only creature I believe we ever punished or prosecuted in our lives. But she was too great a thief to let pass. If she is reformed (and that is easily found out), Mrs. King is to give her a few encouraging lines from me, and the gown; if she continues bad, I have begged her to give it as a wedding-gown to the first young girl of a good Botany Bay character who is married after her arrival.

February 14*th*, 1800.—I am told that the 'Amelia' is to sail in two days now, *cher ami*, and, though very unwell with a bilious complaint which has confined me to my room these three days, I *must* write a few lines in addition to what has gone

[1] Philip Graley King, first Governor of Norfolk Island and Governor of New South Wales.

before, and tell you the *finale* of the affair of our house. I hope it will be a *finale*, and that I shall be able to close my books to grievances—a most uncomfortable style of writing, and one I have regretted I have been obliged to get into with *you*. After having waited a fortnight after the General's marriage for his determination as to what house he chose, during which time the Governor often promised to obtain his decision, at last Mr. Barnard wrote to his Excellency a letter such as he thought he might show to the General to facilitate the conversation. But the Governor declined this, saying he had already 'pressed his reply as much as he could in propriety,' but he thought that Mr. Barnard had a fair right to ask him to decide, and advised him to express his own wishes and sentiments to General Dundas on the subject. Mr. Barnard on this wrote to General Dundas, and received from him a reply saying that Mr. Barnard could remain in *his* house in the Castle until he (General Dundas) wished to occupy it. The implication of this letter was so totally different from what Mr. Barnard had been given to understand from the Governor, that he, amazed, wrote to Sir George, pressing to know the exact state of the case, and beginning to suspect that his Excellency had entangled himself on his first arrival by some hasty promise to Major Erskine for the General, and did not know how to get free so as to satisfy both parties. Sir George replied testily but decisively that the house was *his*, and not

General Dundas's to dispose of, and we might remain in it at his (the Governor's) good pleasure. So here we are going to stay, Mr. Barnard having explained particularly to General Dundas that the house is the Governor's, and he stays in it by *his* leave. I think it likely that the Governor is secretly very angry with General Dundas for assuming so much. But if a man soars too high over the head of another, he must not be surprised if the sun melts his wings and brings him down to the fair level. I am sure I wish he were in this house instead of us, surrounded as we are with his Staff, and that we were at Rondebosch. I wonder, as a military man, that he does not prefer living in the Castle; for the matter of a little barley, corn, and vegetables cannot be an object worthy of his attention, and the command of *all* the houses of Government is a little out of the question. His choice is his own, however, and no fault of ours. Here then ends this business. A little time, I hope, will make all friends. Adieu.

XVII

The Vineyard, Cape of Good Hope:
May 14th, 1800.

IF you knew how often I have thought of getting on with a long letter to you; how often I have postponed it till I should find a better moment; how much I have wished to write to you happily, gaily, foolishly, and as I used to, with nothing in my letters to disturb or annoy you; but how constantly vile little circumstances have arisen to put it out of my power to do so with sincerity, you would almost pity me.

I certainly could say in general terms that we are well, and defer further particulars, but that would not be using you like a friend. I have little doubt that our letters from Cape Colony will be full of circumstances which have been arising here to surprise and agitate a small circle who know not the meaning of some things nor how others will end. The bad terms the General and the Governor are on you will learn from various quarters. On this I might have prophesied almost from the first, but I hoped things might turn out better than I expected. The reverse has been the case. The causes of this

I will endeavour to give, as far as I am able to judge.

With respect to the present Government here, when I tell you that all who compose it are on the best terms with us, civil and rather flatteringly conciliatory, you will not suppose me biassed by any personal disaffection to them when I lament the discreditable shade which some events have lately thrown over Sir George Yonge's administration. I really durst not sooner (from the fear of being unjust) broach even to you what has been here loudly whispered (and what has been too frequently corroborated by a blush that tinged the poor Governor's cheek when pressed by Mr. Barnard), that in some late transactions the hands of Government have not been so clean as they ought to have been. The Dutch have got this idea of the Governor—with what justice God only knows! But so strong an exertion of power has lately been made in favour of a merchant he is unconnected with, giving him not only liberty to import 1,600 slaves, but to land here a supposed cargo (afterwards proved by Captain Campbell in the Court of Justice to be a smuggling transaction, not to use a harsher name to it, the slaves having really been purchased at Mozambique), that it is generally believed that a *douceur* of no small magnitude was given to effect what, had it passed, would have put from 10,000*l.* to 15,000*l.* in the merchant's pocket, whose privateer affected to have taken those slaves. You will naturally say, how happened it that Mr. Barnard, who knew how opposite this was to the ideas of our Government at home, permitted a slave traffic to go on at the Cape, and omitted to state its impropriety to the Governor? Mr. Barnard protested in the strongest terms. He also told the merchant he would oppose it; but he found the Governor deaf to all remonstrance or argument; and as a proof of his being anxious to avoid all further conversation or respectful opposition from Mr. Barnard, he gave the orders for the landing and selling of the slaves, and all necessary arrangements, himself, without bringing them through the Secretary's office, as is customary. One thing you may depend on, that every fair, broad, and proper request invariably goes through the Secretary of the Colony to the Governor; every matter of an unsound or equivocal nature proceeds by the other road, whether in the hopes of obtaining a hasty consent from an inexperienced Governor who will not take time to investigate the matter in question, or whether from other motives, I shall not say. I have sometimes heard Mr. Barnard regret that his power of being of use was so limited, and that it is only after the ill is done his sentiments can appear. But as to all that you know best what is fit. If he has not the means of doing good, he is also free from the vexation of dispute without personal advantage. I can perceive that there seems to be no hurry in either the present Governor, or the past, to send home their accounts. I ask Mr. Barnard frequently when they are to go, expressing my hopes of his being absolved from giving his opinions on past expenses from the time Lord Macartney left the Cape to that when he is required to countersign the papers. But he finds no zeal, no intention of making them up, but on the contrary much dislike of business in the Governor—indeed, to such a degree that the Governor has never read a proclamation or any other paper on the public business of the Colony previous to his arrival.

With respect to the bad terms the Governor and the General are on, I cannot positively affirm whether the blame is on one side only, or whether it is divided. The General skips over the field officers in the garrison, and sends orders to their men without transmitting them through in the regular way, to their great disgust. The Governor sometimes forgets and does the same in trifles; and while the first thinks it presumption in his inferior to be angry, he is offended to the greatest degree with the other for following his example. The Governor reckons himself the head of the army, as well as of everything else here; the General allows him to be only nominally so, and is displeased at his more frequently giving orders respecting the troops than Lord Macartney used to do, who most cautiously avoided small interferences, though he was for ever in his place when it was necessary, the head of all. Perhaps the General might not be so jealous of Sir George as he is, was it not for those around him, who, having got all they could from his Excellency on his first arrival, have now turned their backs on him. We saw the growing coolness, or rather irritability, and conjectured the first moment would be seized that could for rupture. An order for moving a manger where the horses fed, belonging to the cavalry, to the newly repaired barracks in Colonel Cockburn's department, produced a public order from the General conceived in terms so derogatory to Sir George, that military men stared, and feared an arrest would be the consequence. Sir George, though petrified, behaved well on this occasion, by showing a degree of temperance, and wisely gave the General the alternative of asking his pardon or taking the consequences. He, on a little reflection, preferred asking pardon—which he did, as I was told, in the fullest manner—to having the matter sent home, and Sir George gallantly saved his credit with the public in a manner which those who wished to see the General's pride and hastiness humbled called tame, but which we thought wise upon the whole. His Excellency told me that he had promised you to check with mildness any ebullitions which the General's particular temper might throw out, and he had kept his word. Since that time I hear there have been new disputes—fresh offences given and taken; and I hear to-day that the General's *aide-de-camp*, Captain Smith, is going home with dispatches, containing, amongst other things, complaints of his Excellency.

I know not if this is true. I am living out of town, at our little country place which we purchased, built a cottage on, and called 'The Vineyard,' removed from all party work, except working parties in our fields, rooting up of palmite roots, and planting of fir trees and potatoes. I have seen a little of Mrs. Dundas; she is, I think, a judicious woman, and well calculated to increase the popularity of her husband. She is extremely attentive to the world, and it is sensible of it. I think she has more method and better sense in her proceedings than Mrs. Blake, who seems to me to have for her society only the girls that the *aides-de-camp* are in love with, and as they change their loves, so she changes her girls. I see more of her than of Mrs. Dundas, though not much. I think she wishes to convert me to her own use, but the armed neutrality will be of no league. The ladies are, as I foresaw, on terms of ice; the Government House people particularly disliking Mrs. Dundas. I repeat to each every civil word I can which is likely to keep them friends in the Benedick and Beatrice fashion, and I hope to continue well with both, from living much with *neither*.

There has been another strange higgledy-piggledy business going on. It has ended with one person being suspended, and two sent out of the Colony. Mr. Jessop is the first, who goes home till the pleasure of the Administration should be known. Mr. Moss and Mr. Pontardent are the others. I should state the matter very ill if I attempted it in detail. Therefore I shall only say, in general terms, that the Governor granted a permission to certain merchants respecting shipping of certain goods of a nature contrary, as Mr. Jessop thought, to the word and spirit of the Acts of Parliament, or Council, and rights of the East India Company. Mr. Jessop therefore laid his paw on the goods so permitted to be shipped, and, sustained by the opinion of Mr. Moss as Counsel, set the Act of Parliament and his opinion of the Governor's powers of infringing it against the permission and express orders of the Governor.

Mr. Barnard is apt to think that, however wrong Sir George is, or is not, in the first instance Mr. Jessop is bound to obey the Governor, since he only is responsible for the step if wrong. Were not this the case, every man would turn lawyer, and with the Act of Parliament in his hand would act as suited his own translation of it. Mr. Moss is sent off because of the terms in which his opinion is given, and Mr. Pontardent for endeavouring to negotiate a compromise between the parties which would have purchased Mr. Jessop's silence. I don't know the respective merits of these gentlemen, therefore I don't enter into them—I shall only say that the punishment is a heavy one on men glad to escape from home, and earning a livelihood here. But I conclude there is cause for it, though I can scarce think there can be enough to send off the last, who, acting only as a private friend between the parties, was not bound to any particular rigidity of maxim, as a public man is, in matters connected with the laws.

Within these few days some of the troops are

arrived, in a very sickly state, but they will soon get well here. I am told that peace is much talked of at home—I believe in none as yet. Mr. Barnard tells me that you have made 'a glorious speech,' and is to get me the paper. That you should do so is very surprising!!! I hear Lord Loughborough[1] is retiring. I hope his health is not worse than it used to be; my love to him when you see him. Mr. Barnard and I are well at present. I have, however, been more liable this year to little attacks than before, and he swears if I go on so he will pack me off to Europe. Never, never, unless he packs himself off with me. I wish, however, that the conditional leave of absence was in my pocket. It would do me much good, and harm no one, for I really do not think we should make use of it, at least for some time, and would pine much less if we had the power.

Mr. Barnard tells me that the trial of the Dutch prisoners in the Castle is now taking place. I am sorry they were not tried at first—a year and a half's suspense would have been abridged from misery, and much injury avoided to the property of the innocent confined, as well as to the guilty. But the General could resolve on nothing. What a sad pity it is that he cannot determine on anything unless he is in a passion, and then it is a great chance whether is not the wrong way. ' I'll think of it,' ' We shall see,' he cries. Then business of every kind stands still,

[1] The Lord Chancellor, afterwards created the first Earl of Rosslyn.

or rather stood still, except military operations, which are fixed at a minute's thought, without consultation with other officers; and off with the men, without shoes or stockings or without their dinner, hundreds of miles! Perhaps I should not say this; but who will speak out of a person (your nephew) unless such a one as myself? Why has he not Lord Macartney always over him? Though the General eminently disliked Lord Macartney while he stayed, he was awed by his superior abilities, and he now much prefers him to the present master.

I am this morning told by some military men that the Governor's household, all except Sir George, will be recalled in consequence of representations the General is sending home, in which case they affirm the General will succeed to the Government as Governor. Certainly every good fortune which could attend the General I should rejoice at, save that which would make him the head of a peaceable and well-regulated society. He is not calculated for civil life, though he may be a brave officer and an honest man. But too sure it is, that while he reigned over us disaffection in all the departments, feuds, and war took place, and every sort of personal disgust was given. However, I fancy the good folk here need not be afraid of his having again the reins of government, as, however much Sir George may be suspected of loving a *douceur*, it requires far broader proof than it is likely ever can come forward, for a recall to take place; the more so as Sir George would be without provision at home. I protest I should be very sorry if anything of the sort were to take place; he and all his household, his niece Mrs. Blake, Mr. Blake, and Colonel Cockburn are very civil to us, and I feel great goodwill to them, though I do not think they proceed on good plans.

At first Sir George did me the honour of consulting me on various things; and I gave my opinion as ingenuously, where I thought it my duty, as Gil Blas gave his to the Archbishop of Toledo. Of course it had the same effect. My counsels being sometimes unpalatable, I was soon suspended. I advised him against a select concert on which he had set his heart, to the exclusion of all the Cape Dutch, except a favoured fifty, and the Fiscal did the same. I told him it would be fatal to the peace of society, and Mr. Barnard thinks he has not quite forgiven me for having been in the right. But he is so well bred and friendly in his manner that he buys me off. This is the full account of everything as it now stands.

I long to hear from you of all things. You bid me continue to write to you unreservedly, which I do in the amplest manner, giving you my thoughts where I think they can be of any use to you, unprejudiced accounts of what is going on in a corner of the world you are interested in, in the full confidence of friendship. God bless all at Wimbledon, dear Lady Jane first, after your sweet self. If it was not for Margaret I should not know half enough about you, for the newspapers tell me only fibs; at least I think it very improbable that the State will consent to your retiring, a lazy peer, no longer the sonorous voice of wisdom giving the law in the House of Commons to John Bull! If, however, you find such scenes absolutely fatal to your health, retire from them in a degree by living in Scotland till such time as the Temple of Janus is shut. Then open the Temple of Dunira and let us, I pray, into some corner of it when we return from the Cape.

XVIII

*The Vineyard, Cape of Good Hope:
June 1st, 1800.*

I WROTE to you so very lately, my dear Friend, that I have not much to say now. However, I feel so delighted to have a page or two with you free from any grumblings or vexation, that I seize the pen with the greater alacrity—perhaps with additional alacrity—from having had yesterday a visit that gave me satisfaction—Mrs. Dundas, not alone, but accompanied by the General. I was happy Mr. Barnard was at home. Whether the General came of himself, or whether she brought him, we shall not inquire too closely, but I rather suspect the latter. It is this trait in her conduct which particularly pleases me: she sways her husband to conciliatory and right things, instead of keeping him aloof, as his men friends did. This is not her character with the other party—I mean the Government House people; but I must judge for myself, and I lean to the opinion of her being temperate, civil, and judicious. If she continues so, I shall strongly wish to call her friend instead of acquaintance, and shall be delighted if, through her means, some little faults in her husband's temper may be wholly smoothed over, if not eradicated, which would be of solid use in a character which has not one mean or dishonourable point in it. The General is really a little of a character. It is impossible he can have wholly forgotten what has been passing between him and Mr. Barnard, but he entered the room yesterday as a man would do who had no notion that another had any cause to resent any part of his conduct. I rubbed my eyes and fancied I had been asleep; however, such is the power that old impressions have over me, such the goodwill I have always felt to him for his own sake as a Dundas, and such the double, triple portion as so near a connection of yours, that when I looked at him I said to myself, ' Oh, what a pity that you cannot be good-humoured and friendly with us all without interruption; and how vexed I am that I have felt myself necessitated to growl at you to your uncle without telling you I have.' If I see anything like heartiness continue, however, tell him I will; nothing shall keep me silent but fear, and if that fear blows by and kindness is allowed to grow again, I will make a clean breast with him, shake hands, and begin again on a new score. To me the joy and comfort of society consists of loving and of being beloved by those one lives amongst, whether Britons or Hottentots. I see slights with difficulty, as I look for none; but seeing, I feel them with deep vexation which I am convinced drives a nail in my coffin. Such a frame of mind is too painful for me not to be ready to throw it off, and to forgive—ay, from the very bottom of my heart, whenever I can find a loophole to be happy again. And this is just the position I stand in now. I long to read 'Upon my soul you are good people, I believe, after all,' in the eyes of those abominable Scarlet Coats who have so worked us; could I find that sentence in every pair of eyes around me I should not mind staying here as much longer as you would think for the benefit of the Colony. But ill used by the above folks for a length of time, my heart died within me at the prospect of remaining fixed at the Cape, where it was quite frozen and chilled up with cold looks.

Now I'll begin again, sanguine fool that I am, to hope better things, to give all another fair trial, and also (aided by Mrs. Dundas, if she will help me) try to cement better together the head and shoulders of the body politic—that is, the Governor and the General—than they have been of late. You will think I have been reading my Bible lately, as I perceive I am making the statue of Darius out of the component materials here. In that statue the head was made of 'pure gold.' I know not how far the allusion holds true with Sir George; it has been thought, as I told you, that gold was in his head, perhaps from being so long at the head of the Mint![1]

[1] Sir George Yonge was Master of the Mint from 1794 to 1799, before he was appointed Governor of the Cape of Good Hope.

But if his head had been made of gold, I think Lady Yonge would have tried to melt it before now; in such a case the woman who adds height to her husband's head certainly exalts his horn—when it is a golden one. But I am talking nonsense! If Mr. Barnard and I could get this same golden head and the silver shoulders to jar less and fit better, it would be very comfortable to us: the pedestal, which, being composed of a little of the inferior metals, as well as a mixture of the equal, is not strong enough to bear much fighting. As yet Mr. Barnard has, without appearing in it, been of some little use by becalming advice when the Governor's eyebrow was cocked, and I would fain hope there will be no more wranglings now till the return of Captain Smith, the General's *aide-de-camp*, with a good scold, I hope, to both of them. I declare I think they might be very happy here in their departments if that foolish thirst for supremacy, and inattention to the thing below them (I talk of military matters), did not step in.

For the last four months, as I told you, I have remained constantly in the country, 'like a mouse in a mill,' till the ladies should get righted in their *berths*, as they say of ships—and why not of ladyships? But I shall shortly go to Cape Town to pay my mite to society, now that I perceive it begins to live for me. I believe it is a pretty policy on some occasions to make oneself scarce. By the bye, there is a new scheme with which the Governor is bitten, and which (like the affair of the select concert) will probably fail to the ground from its not being on a well-judged plan. 'Tis a theatre, all boxes, no pit, each box to cost 24*l*. a year, and to hold six subscribers, for twelve nights only; consequently it is on too dear a plan to suit the pockets of subalterns, and yet they look for the performers from amongst the military. We have a box, of course, but take no subscribers, giving away our tickets as we please to our friends. Thirty-two boxes are subscribed for; but large as this sum is for this small place, it is found too little to repair an old pottery belonging to Government for that purpose, which by estimate (the scale of Sir George's ideas being always too much *en grand*) would cost 2,500*l*.

His idea of a theatre was grounded on a little piece got up by Doctor Somers, physician to the Army, in the Military Hospital, which hospital his wife, who is a fine-spoken woman, will not call *hospital* but *Sea-line*! It was really very well, however, upon the whole. The piece was one of Foote's called 'Teasle'; the Doctor himself acted 'Lady Bentweazle' in a very Lady Bentweazle-like manner, Major Glegg was 'Carmine,' and Colonel Barlow was inimitable as 'Puff.' I had an old shilling Paris-plaster horse, which acted the equestrian statue of Marcus Aurelius, the figure only wanting; and a large bronze Venus in paper, out of my stores, was dug out of the Herculaneum for the occasion. The Doctor spoke an ode, rather of, than to, the passions, and Mrs. Somers spoke a prologue of her own composing. Altogether it was very good, innocent fun, and much more harmless than horse-racing, drinking, or any other amusement that could be introduced to bring people together in such a place as this. Sir George, enchanted with the entertainment, instantly began to invent a mode for continuing it, arranged the plan of this theatre, and brought forth the bantling scheme, a full-grown arrangement. We all subscribed to it, though we foresaw the difficulties likely to present themselves. No sooner was this first point gained, and a prospect had of a sufficient number of male performers, than the gentlemen actors declared half off, unless ladies would join in the cause. This idea was secretly one of Sir George's, too; and thus supported, he came forwards with all his power and all his persuasion to prevail on us all to assist. Mrs. Somers, a pretty Mrs. Kelso, and one or two other ladies hinted themselves ready to act if I would, or if Mrs. Dundas or Mrs. Blake would. The last said she would if I would (knowing that I would not); the other said nothing. I told the Governor frankly that if he had a theatre in his own house, and laid his commands on me to do anything to prove my desire of contributing to his entertainment, I was ready, providing the part given me was sufficiently insignificant, but that I had neither talents nor memory for more. As to acting on any theatre where money was to be paid for admission, or any theatre except one in his house, I whispered my fixed refusal. But everyone is at me on the score of my being able to sing; as to being able to act, I make no doubt I could if I were to try. But I am very sure that I *won't*, and that if I could suppose I was to start forward the first of actresses, it would not make me the less resolved against what it is want of sense to propose to me.

Whether this matter will fall to the ground altogether, or whether the Governor will fit up a little theatre in his own house (which in point of expense would be a twopenny matter), I can't tell. If he does the latter, all the ladies are ready to join me in offering to do something, to dance a cotillon between the acts, be chorus or orange girls, or anything to prove their good-humour. But we are in great hopes that the trouble this would give his Excellency (which he is not fond of taking except in his own way) will prevent our offers from being accepted. We have had many female recruits from the arrival of the 34th and 22nd Regiments—some of them acquisitions to society. Colonel Dickins was an old Westminster schoolfellow of Mr. Barnard's, and has married a woman reckoned to be well-bred and pleasing, but she is ten years older than I am, if that is possible! It seems to be the way of Westminster School to marry Charmers of the upper forms;[1] however, if it answers as well in *her* instance as it does

---

[1] Another allusion to Lady Anne's being many years older than her husband.

in another I know of, she has no cause of regret. I am much pleased with the arrival of this colleague in seniority. I before stood unrivalled; now I am a chicken by comparison. They live at our house in the Castle, or, to speak more accurately, at the house we occupy there, till they can fix themselves. General Dundas has lent the Lieutenant-Governor's house to Colonel and Mrs. Hamilton, and lives in town this winter, so we shall have a good female society in the Castle. There is a Colonel Mercer and his wife who have been lately staying with us in the country also; her name before marriage was Miss Clarinda O'Grady. She is rather handsome, but the longest woman I ever saw in all my life, and wears a pair of seven-league boots with which she steps across a room of any dimensions. Her Colonel is four inches taller than she; they measure twelve feet seven inches together. It is the fashion to laugh at Clarinda here, as uncouth and unpolished; but Mr. Barnard and I have an odd tendency to like her ingenuous bluntness, and if on further acquaintance it proves to be honest frankness, I shall prize it as a large web of a rare coarse stuff, the pattern of which she gives one the first moment one is in her company. She was married but a month before she stepped across the sea in her boots. There are four or five other ladies, but the two I have mentioned are the principal ones. All bring me a quantity of fibs about you, your insisting on retiring, your peerage, your pension, and give me many long conversations between you and his Majesty.[1] I believe nothing I hear, exactly as I hear it, but I believe in that tiny quantity of truth which makes the basis for falsehood. You won't desert the House of Commons till you have made a peace, or till there is some one found in some degree equal to fill your place, and where is he hid at present? Everyone here is full of the approaching peace; I do not credit that either—I wish I did; it would give me a delightful vista of hope of seeing home before I die.

I have letters yesterday from Lord Wellesley *alias* Mornington.[2] He writes in health and in spirits, says he is often proud, sometimes melancholy; that he affects to be happy but sighs for home, though he does not conceive he has any chance of returning till everything is fixed where he is on a firm and permanent foundation. The large pension that I hear has been voted to him will add further joy and astonishment to that thunderbolt of prosperity which has almost at once struck him; he has a mind to taste all its power, and I really think a heart to make the best use of it. Knowing him as intimately as I do, I had

---

[1] Dundas differed both from the King and Pitt about the Egyptian campaign, but had his way, and the event justified his policy. The King subsequently toasted him as 'The Minister who planned the expedition to Egypt, and in doing so had the courage to resist his King.' On Pitt's resignation in March 1801, Dundas resigned the Office of Secretary for War, and also his position as President of the Board of Control, which gave him influence over Indian and Colonial affairs. He, however, gave a general support to Addington, and accepted a peerage from him in 1802, being created Viscount Melville and Baron Dunira.

[2] He had now been created Marquess of Wellesley.

a great latent wish, rather than a hope, to hear of some wee-bit title being in his patent to gild over the disgrace of illegitimacy to his eldest son, who I am told is promising and amiable to a great degree. Nothing short of such a deed as Lord Wellesley has done [1] could, I dare say, draw such a mark of the Royal favour; but I declare it does not strike me as being so strong a one as the title given to Lady Cecil Hamilton. I am sorry for that poor girl. Married to a different sort of man, I dare say she would have behaved better. I hear Margaret is to be married to him, and have written her a letter of condolence. 'Sister Anne, Sister Anne,' would be very sorry to see her married to such a Bluebeard. I must, however, say that if he were to propose it to her, I should think it the wisest thing he ever did in his life for his family; and if she were to accept, I should think —she had better let it alone.

The weather here begins to be very bad—it rains *seas*, but I wish to remain here at the Vineyard till we can get this little place quite finished and comfortable, in case of our remaining another season in it, which I would fain hope would be the extent of our stay. Will it, do you think? I suppose this will be a gay winter at the Cape: a subscription ball, a concert, besides three houses to give good things —the Governor's, General Dundas's, and ours. I tell the two ladies that I am entitled to be lazy now that such duties devolve more regularly on them. But,

[1] The final victory over Tippoo and the fall of Seringapatam.

as I before said, I shall still pay my mite to public and private cheerfulness. I hear the Governor's society runs very young just now. I fancy he takes himself for King David, by his fondness for having a little girl of fourteen or fifteen on each side of him. Half a dozen of such compose the evening parties, and they dance, and he dances, to a hand-organ, the little girls laughing (I cannot say in their sleeves, as there is nothing now but bare elbows). Colonel Cockburn is generally in love with from six to twelve of them at a time, and as he is very inconstant the Governor has a good chance of seeing all the young Beauties the Cape affords at his house in a short time. He takes care, however, to let me understand that he is a flirt, and can't think of marrying without the consent of Sir George, who intends never to consent, so all is above board. Sir Roger Curtis has given over the chase of the fair Baumgardt. I fancy she won't like this; she never was left before for any other person, though often when her swains went home. But report says that he has attached himself to another frigate more to his mind; and as I often see him riding at anchor, gallantly escorting on horseback a pretty married woman, we are inclined to believe it. Thus you have all my Cape news—one piece still remains, but it is no scandal. I believe you will in due course of time have a little relation in the General's family—it appears to be so, and I'm glad of it. And now, having finished my seventh page—God bless you both.

June 5th.—No, sure! Is it possible that a leave of absence to Mr. Barnard is actually sent to us by your own dear self? This piece of news comes in two letters to me by the 'Triton,' but it comes unsupported by anything from yourself, from my sisters, or from our friendly peer, Lord Macartney. I must not, therefore, *quite* believe in it till I see it, though the manner in which it is mentioned carries the face of truth on it.

Well!—with a sigh—if it is so, we will receive it by some ships not yet come in, and will thank you for it with all our hearts and souls. It will make our future voluntary residence here the more cheery and light that we may shorten it at pleasure, as health or any very strong compulsory reason may govern. But as things at present stand here, neither Mr. Barnard nor I should reckon we behaved handsomely to you if we availed ourselves of it now. From a variety of reasons Mr. Barnard has cause to suppose that he has been, and may be, of use in more respects than one; and composed as the Government here is, at present, and ill-assorted as the jarring individuals are to each other, he thinks that he should ill repay your goodness if he permitted personal gratification to take the lead of duty.

June 25th.—More ships are come in—but no more letters for poor me. I suppose all that I am now most desirous of receiving are gone to India to be returned to me from England about a year hence. Somebody, I forget whom, says: 'Philosophy is a fine horse in the stable, but apt to tire on the road.' Have I not need, my dear good soul, of a stout palfrey of that kind at present? But I will not repine; they'll come when we shall feel ourselves more at liberty to act upon them; meantime I hope we shall receive duplicates. Write me a few lines, I pray, my dear friend, on the receipt of this letter, as it is possible this leave may never reach us at all, if it is gone on to India. Write them kindly, and in charity with me, pray, forgiving me for all my impertinences, else I shall sail home (even if you permit me to sail) in bad spirits, and may perhaps jump into the sea from the blue devils.

The first Agricultural Meeting took place a few days ago. The Governor was President; the Lieutenant-Governor Vice-President. Mr. Barnard would not step forward as the other Vice-President, declining his chance of election to that dignity in favour of some Dutch gentleman, whose knowledge of the country, climate, and usages of the farmers make him better qualified to lead. Four thousand dollars was subscribed to the plan at the first meeting, and more, I believe, daily comes in. So the Governor for once has reason to be pleased with his scheme, which in truth is the only one which has any reference to the real improvement of the country. Poor soul, he seems to have proceeded hitherto in the idea that laying out its funds on superficial matters is improving the place.

This page is like a newspaper. That reminds

me—the Governor is resolved to have one here. If it answers as the printing of an Almanac did in the Dutch time it will be droll. The printer made a fortune of *two shillings* by it; each of the four districts took one at sixpence—all the inhabitants read or copied out of that one!

XIX

*The Vineyard, Cape of Good Hope:
February 16th, 1801.*

THANKS to some anxious reason Lord Wellesley has for sending off a quick sailing-vessel to England, with orders not to be an hour beyond three days at the Cape, I have an unexpected opportunity of writing to my dearest friend. An event too important to this Colony has taken place (or at least a well authenticated report of it) for me to be silent at present. Nothing can exceed the wisdom of your recall of Sir George. It is a measure infinitely judicious, and its strength and untemporising decision came like a thunderbolt on the discontented Dutch, who were beginning to talk lightly of a Government which had sent them such a head. But the Governor's recall made several of them break out into a sort of astonished gratitude and respect for the care manifested by the Home Government for Cape interests at the wide distance of 6,000 miles, which had prompted so firm a step. The change indeed is grounded on not above the fourth part of the improper things which have since taken place to have grounded a change upon. To say the truth, transported as both Mr. Barnard and I were when the news reached us, we were (at least I was) very much astonished at the right radical reform which you had administered to the evil. Sir George has always buzzed it into my ears that he was a particular favourite of the King, and how his Majesty had made it a point that he should accept of this Government, that I had feared a part of this might be true, and would influence you to more consideration for the man than his conduct deserved. I had rather expected that something of a Council would be appointed to govern along with him, more for the above reason than for any other. But there seems not a doubt, even to my addle-pate, that the present method is the best, as Sir George would not have submitted to colleagues in judgment. We all rejoice in his foolish, faulty reign being over.

I wonder if you will appoint a new Governor, and who he will be; on it so much depends.[1] Lord Macartney's strong abilities, which appeared even in common conversation, his acumen, and his *l'usage du monde*, were so suited to his station, that few men could have succeeded him, however able, who might not have lost on the comparison. But this poor man came after, who possesses nothing but civility, the bow born of a long apprenticeship at Court, and a star. A strong man now would step forward like a diamond who has had at his back a foil.

[1] Lord Glenbervie was appointed, but when the Addison Ministry came into power his appointment was cancelled, and he never came out to the Cape.

Certainly, in one sense, whoever succeeds our poor old Governor will owe him something. He has been for his successor a most active overseer; instead of finding a dirty old house with a perpendicular staircase, up which Lord Macartney hopped, gout and all, like a parrot to his perch, he will find rooms well painted and papered with papers of my Lady Yonge's own choosing, an excellent staircase, the fellow of Lady Buckingham's in St. James's Square; and instead of gardens productive only of weeds they are now full stocked with everything, even fishponds, made at great expense (we shan't talk of that now). Everything, in short, which could be wished for, Sir George has provided, and left nothing to pay, at least nothing by the new Administration. This is being in luck; nor let the great saving of patience be forgotten and of constitution employed in scolding, and the employment of time in being the overseer of workmen.

No official accounts are as yet received from home. At first Sir George was, I hear, very much thunderstruck. He said the next day to Mr. Barnard that he could not comprehend what part of his conduct could have given displeasure at home; and to be sure he had no reason to believe in a report which came unauthenticated, but that Lady Yonge's letters gave him some cause to put faith in it. However, as nothing now makes much impression on his memory, I daresay he will soon believe that he has had an ugly dream of recall only. He currently talked here the other day (at a dinner to which he had in a fit of graciousness invited himself and a large party) of what he was to do three months hence. I hope he will not in the meantime do anything difficult to be undone afterwards. Some fears of this kind, I fancy, made General Dundas ask to have a conference with Mr. Barnard t'other day, who from every cause was happy to have it, and they there laid their heads together how to prevent some things from taking place which would put a new Governor to the trouble of undoing, and are better avoided. Mr. Barnard told the General how earnestly and reiteratedly he had argued against these and various other matters, not only in conversation but by pen and ink, perhaps in too strong a manner for civility, but not stronger than the necessity of the case demanded. The General approved. I own myself very much pleased to see Mr. Barnard standing, almost the only person who has neither asked or obtained any favour from Sir George—nay, who, pressed and solicited to name but his wishes, whether for grant of land or anything else, has never been tempted into acquiescence, however glad he might have been to have obtained such a grant from a more respected hand. I should really be glad to learn for certain whether poor Sir George has actually lodged in his own pocket any of the *douceurs* returned for favours conferred. Much the larger part of society here believe that he has. But some are of a contrary opinion, and I am apt to class with those who think that his greedy secretary, Mr. Blake, using a female influence which it is supposed has power over him, prevailed on the Governor to do many things for their benefit, which I traced to the weakness of a very old man for the person about him. I suppose something must clear this up in the course of a little time.

With respect to our movements; we shall not now leave the Colony for some months, until things are more settled. Sir George wishes to remain in Government House until he can sell off his things, which requires a few weeks. When this is over Mr. Barnard will ask him to remain with us until he sails. Poor man, he is good-natured though weak, and one feels a pity for those grey locks which he might have laid down with honour and peace at the bottom of the Table Mountain if he had had a set of more disinterested people about him. Alas! those round him can make him do anything. I'll give you a whimsical instance. A person in the Corn Board, lately established here somewhat on the plan of Joseph's in Egypt, as granaries against scarcity, complained sadly yesterday that Sir George ordered the Board to occupy and pay rent for the warehouses underneath the playhouse, instead of remaining in the premises they had already taken. Although they have remonstrated by letter, stating that they have 3,000 square feet more in space, at 360 rix dollars less rent, their remonstrance has had no effect, for all the Governor's favourites and household are subscribers to this same playhouse; so the Board is ordered to take the storehouses.

The heat of the weather at present is very great—everybody is annoyed by it. The thermometer is 104 at Cape Town in the shade. At our country house there is ten degrees of difference. The 61st Regiment, or part of it, embarks to-morrow. The last troops that have come out have all landed much more healthy than the former ones, probably from having excellent accommodation. I will now release my dearest friend, with every deep and kind wish for his happiness, and that no ailings may destroy the fine habit of good health which has been habitual to him. With kind love to Lady Jane, I remain, yours affectionately,

ANNE BARNARD.

XX

THE foregoing was the last letter that Lady Anne Barnard wrote from the Cape to Lord Melville—at least it is the last preserved in the Melville MSS. On Pitt's resignation, in March 1801, Dundas resigned the office of Secretary for War, and in the following May resigned his position at the Board of Control. Lord Hobart was appointed in his place, and the affairs of the Cape passed into other hands. Dundas, however, gave a general support to the Addington Ministry, and accepted a peerage (Viscount Melville) from Addington at the end of the year. One result of the accession of the Addington Ministry to power was that no new Governor was sent out to the Cape in place of Sir George Yonge; and the administration of the Colony was again placed in the hands of the Lieutenant-Governor (General Dundas) who was appointed Acting-Governor. The reason for this was that Addington was negotiating for a peace with France, in which the cession of the Cape formed an important consideration. The preliminaries were signed on October 1st, 1801, and a definite treaty was signed at Amiens the following March between Great Britain, France, and the Batavian Republic, as Holland was then called. By this treaty the Cape of Good Hope was ceded to the Dutch. Accordingly, in February 1803 the English flag was hauled down, a Dutch garrison replaced the British troops, and General Dundas transferred the government to the Dutch High Commissioner, De Mist.

Lady Anne Barnard remained at the Cape until January 1802, when she returned to England. Mr. Barnard came home some months later, when the civil business of the Colony was transferred to its new masters. Lady Anne was perhaps the only member of the English Colony whose departure was generally regretted by the Dutch. Her hospitality, her warm heart, and general desire to conciliate, had gained her many friends among them, and a large party of Dutch, headed by the Fiscal, came to the quay to see her off. Her five years' residence at the Cape showed what could be done by tact and good feeling to break down the divisions between the two nationalities.

The cession of the Cape to the Dutch is not pleasant reading. A comic relief in this somewhat humiliating page of our Colonial history was afforded, unintentionally, by Sir George Yonge, the last Governor of the first British occupation of South Africa. His career, subsequent to his recall, forms a sequel to Lady Anne's letters. He was recalled suddenly by Lord Melville in a despatch dated

January 14th, 1801, and ordered to return home immediately. He asked for time to wind up his affairs, but through the ill-will of the Lieutenant-Governor this was refused him. The Proclamation was issued immediately, and he and his household had to quit the Castle at once. The ex-Governor then applied to Sir Roger Curtis, the Admiral commanding at the Cape, for a man-of-war to take him to St. Helena, but this also was refused, and he was left waiting—the very emblem of fallen greatness—in a lodging at Cape Town until he could find an ordinary ship to take him home.

Meantime Lord Hobart, who had become Secretary of State, instituted an inquiry into Yonge's conduct at the Cape. A commission was appointed, with General Dundas at its head. After a lengthy inquiry, Blake, Sir George Yonge's private secretary, and Cockburn, his principal *aide-de-camp*, were accused in the report of gross malpractices, such as trade in licences, monopolies, and giving permission for slaves to be sold in the Colony. They also accused Yonge of being cognisant of the same. This report was sent home to England, where Yonge had now arrived, but no action was taken upon it, possibly because the Cape was so soon to be ceded to the Dutch, more probably because the ex-Governor stood high in the King's favour. We find Yonge writing to Lord Hobart (July 26th, 1802)[1] that he had had an audience of the King at Weymouth, and:

[1] The Records of Cape Colony.

'I had the honour of reporting to his Majesty the state of the Colony over which I had been Governor, and the whole of my conduct during my residence there. I found his Majesty perfectly well informed of every particular concerning it beforehand, and had the happiness to be assured of his entire approbation of my conduct and services.' Grown bolder by this mark of the Royal favour, Yonge followed up his letter by a demand to Lord Hobart for his expenses home, lodging, etc., amounting to over 1,000*l*. No notice was taken of this application; but the King consoled his fallen favourite by a grant of rooms in Hampton Palace, where he lived until he died at the ripe old age of eighty-one.

This book covers only the first English occupation of the Cape, but we are unwilling to end it by leaving the Colony in Dutch hands. The rule of the Batavian Republic was very brief. Less than three months after the cession of the Colony, war broke out again between Great Britain and the Netherlands, and no one doubted that the English would take possession of the Cape at the first opportunity. On the 1st March, 1803, the Dutch celebrated by a public thanksgiving the cession to them of the Cape. On the 4th January, 1806, the English fleet again anchored in Table Bay. The British troops, under General Baird, were quickly landed, and, after an engagement known as the Battle of Blueberg, in which the Dutch were defeated, the Batavian Governor capitulated. General Baird took formal possession of Cape Town, and a few weeks later the last representative of the Batavian Republic set sail for Holland. For a few years the Cape was ruled by the English as a conquered territory under temporary occupation by the Governor (Lord Caledon), but when the European war came to an end a convention was signed in London, August 1814, whereby Cape Colony was formally handed over to England by the Netherlands, and under English rule it has since remained.